ME

&

ELLAN VANNIN

A wartime childhood on the Isle of Man

ANN MOORE

Second Edition

Published by
Eyelevel Books
Worcester, England

ISBN: 9781902528410

Author's note:

This is a personal recollection of childhood spent in the Isle of
Man during war years, originally written for my family until it was
suggested that it might have a wider appeal. I should like to
thank Steve and Colin Brown from The Manx Experience and
Jon, Sarah Christian and Dawn Maddrell, Colin Russell for their
help. We all know that memory can play tricks and if I
inadvertently offend anyone I knew, or make a mistake in facts
as I believed them to be, then I can only apologise. My regard
for the island and its people is too great for me to ever wish to
cause offence.

Designed and typeset by Eyelevel Books, Worcester.
www.eyelevelbooks.co.uk

For a much loved family past and present.

The Manx National Anthem

(Arrane Ashoonagh Dy Vannin)

The first of eight verses, words by W.H.Gill, translated by J.J. Kneen and sung to an adaptation of a traditional Manx Air:

O Halloo nyn ghooie,
O Chliegeen ny s'bwaaie,
Ry ghedyn er ooir aalin Yee,
Ta dt' Ardstoyl Reill-Thie
Myr Baarool er ny hoie
Dy reayll shin ayns seyrsnys
*   as shee.*

O Land of our birth,
O gem of God's earth,
O island so strong and so fair,
Built firm as Barrule,
Thy throne of Home Rule
Makes us free as thy sweet
*   mountain air.*

THE ISLE OF MAN

(NOT TO SCALE)

Chapter 1

At last it had arrived – the day we were to set off on an adventure! Well, that's what it felt like to me, the city born, seven-year old daughter and only child of loving parents. I watched Mother as she mumbled through the list in her hand.

'Train tickets, money for the boat, Service payment book to prove we're going to see Daddy, identity cards, ration books, gasmasks and Daddy's alarm clock so he won't be late for school!' I giggled. Daddy in school and here was I going on holiday when I should have been there too. My best friend Sylvia was green with envy. She was a bit older than I was and her father was in the Services too, in the Army, but she couldn't go to see him, so I'd promised to bring her a present. I enjoyed Sylvia's friendship. She seemed to know so much more about life than I did. And she could spit cherry or plum stones at a target with great accuracy.

But the best part of the whole thing was that I would see my father again.

Above, left: the author with her parents and precious doll Rosie. Cheshire 1940
Top right: author's father as a young soldier in the Guards.
Above, right: Royal Air Force Volunteer, June 1941

For the last two years he'd been away from us too often and I'd missed his bedtime stories and games and our fun arguments over whose turn it was to eat the crispy skin off the edge of the rice pudding dish. Mother always got cross with us and then Daddy would pull a funny face. She didn't realise we argued just to tease her. I missed him because when he was a Fireman he'd been sent to Liverpool to fight the fires in the blitz. Then, frustrated by trying to clear up the mess left by bombs, he said he wanted to be more active in the fight against the enemy. So he'd become a volunteer Observer Navigator in the Royal Air Force and that took him away from us too. But then that was the sort of person he was. Photographs on the sideboard showed that: Daddy in the Army as a young boy (younger than he said he was when he joined up), a member of a Cavalry regiment who served on the northwest frontier of India; and later representing the Kings Dragoon Guards in the boxing ring.

But now, in this happy summer of 1942, we were going to join him for a few weeks in the Isle of Man where, as a member of No 5 Bombing and Gunnery School, he was completing his RAF training. Then he'd join a Bomber Command Squadron somewhere as a Navigator, and we'd return home to our tall terraced house in Cheshire until the war was over and we'd all be together again.

He'd told us something about our destination in his letters, but couldn't say too much because, as Government posters reminded us, 'Careless Talk Costs Lives'.

His RAF station at Jurby was in the north of a small independent island, 33 miles long and 13 across, set in the middle of the Irish Sea. Since it was a relatively safe place away from big cities and bombing raids, Daddy thought it would be nice for us to spend a little time together because he missed us as much as we did him. He'd described the island to me in his last letter. He always included a note for 'Miss Ann' with Mother's letters, even if it was only a little drawing.

He wrote that it was a beautiful place with '... lots of rabbits running about in the fields and little lambs that let you stroke their noses ... and lots of big aeroplanes like the one with the big glass nose where I sit and look out,' and he'd added, '... I often see kiddies in the playgrounds of schools waving to us as we pass over the school'.

And now at last, after a crowded train journey, full of soldiers and unhappy looking people, we were actually steaming our way across the Irish Sea to be with him.

I sat on a coil of rope in the middle of the deck with my big doll Rosie and a book. It was peaceful in the sun with the gentle sway of the boat and the splashing of the waves. Our two-year old dog, Ruff, sat between Mother and me, sniffing the air. Our neighbour, Mrs Booth, had agreed to look after our three cats, but couldn't manage him as well, so he'd come with us. 'He'll enjoy a country holiday,' said Mother. When he was a puppy she'd rescued him from a small boy who was trying to push him down a drain outside our house. She brought him back to life, and when she'd cleaned him up and rubbed him with a towel, his fur looked untidy and rough, so that's what we called him.

Suddenly Ruff stood up, shook himself, and pulling his lead from beneath Mother's foot, he pattered over to the ship's rail and peered down into the water.

'No! Ruff, Stay!' Mother shouted as she hurried after him. She'd forgotten that he'd never 'stay' anywhere if he didn't want to. Then, as she grabbed the lead, she called, 'Ann, look! There's the island.'

And sure enough the faint outline of a coast and hills was gradually coming into view. In time we would find that the Isle of Man was – still is – a place of tranquil, unspoilt countryside and a few towns; of fern-clad hills painted with yellow gorse and purple heather; of sandy beaches and secret coves, rivers and pretty glens. It enjoys fishing, agriculture and tourism, and clean fresh air free from industrial smoke. Twice invaded by Vikings who gave it Tynwald, the oldest continuous parliament in the world, it has many place-names with roots in the language of Scandinavia. But its countrymen are still basically Celtic, clinging to their history and folk-law, cautious, thrifty and unforthcoming. A Manxman will carry on a pleasant conversation with a stranger, nodding slowly and listening well, but he will give away nothing of himself.

But of course none of this we knew – nor did we want to. We were too intent on arriving and being reunited with my father. As yet couldn't even see the high barrier of wire frames imprisoning the tall boarding houses along the two-mile sweep of Douglas Bay.

The four-hour sea journey over and our little family complete once more, we walked along the quay, past fishing boats in the harbour, until at last we

reached a redbrick Victorian railway station. Two carriages stood patiently behind a fat little engine steaming quietly to itself against one of the platforms.

'Here we are then,' said my father opening a door. 'In you jump.' I bounced down on to one of the fat tapestry seats and a faint cloud of dust danced in the sunlight. Then as Daddy stretched up to put our cases in a rack on the wooden wall above my head – it looked like a long string shopping bag – I noticed faded coloured pictures below it; but before I could examine them, the engine gave a loud shriek, the carriage shuddered, and we began the last leg of our journey.

Off we went, creaking and swaying through the countryside, towards the north of the island and Ramsey, a small sea-side town less than twenty miles away. It was just four miles from Sulby, the village where Daddy had found the bungalow which for a few weeks would be our holiday home. Hedges and fields hurried past as the train hurled us round corners. Ferns and flowers grew by the side of the narrow track, dainty blue harebells beneath towering foxgloves and bright yellow ragwort. Then the train shrilled its whistle and drew to a halt against the short platform of Union Mills, bright with flowers and little white statues set among the leaves.

'Look at the stationmaster,' said Daddy, 'see the rose in his buttonhole? They say he'll give you a shilling if you ever see him without a flower in his jacket.' But I never did. To the day he died, the man always wore a flower from his station garden.

We rattled on, shrilling our way in and out of

small country stations, where guards blew whistles and waved little green flags to send us on our way again. Sometimes we saw fields of sheep looking freshly laundered, but they were too busy nibbling grass to notice the train. Then I saw the sea sparkling in the distance and staggered across to the window which faced the coast.

'That's the sea you've just crossed,' said my father. 'But quick – look! Do you see that very tall stone standing in the middle of the field?' I was just in time to catch a glimpse before we rounded another bend. 'Well,' he went on, 'always look at it carefully whenever you pass and you may see it move. It sometimes turns when the wind's in the right direction.' Then as I stared at him in disbelief, he grinned and added, 'the Isle of Man is a beautiful, magical place, full of fairies and little people, you know. Just you wait and see.'

Chapter 2

Tar plopped in little puddles by the side of the lane. As we left Sulby station to make our way along a shimmering road, it oozed, black and shiny, trying to anchor my sandals to the hot gravel. Clutching Rosie I trotted along behind my parents deep in conversation. Everything was quiet and still, breathless even though the hot June day would soon be drawing to a close. There seemed to be nothing except the sun beating down from a fierce blue sky, high dusty hedges and that shiny river of tar. Here and there a few cows munched lazily in roadside fields, swishing tails against flies or dozing in the shade of a tree. Nothing moved. Nobody appeared. Even the birds were still. Only the sound of Mother's high heels disturbed a silence which I felt I dare not break. This country lane was a world away from the busy streets and terraced houses we had left early that morning. This new world seemed to watch and wait. It was all so strange and new and exciting.

'Nearly there,' said Daddy over his shoulder. 'Come on, keep up!'

By now we were passing occasional cottages and a few houses set in neat gardens. Then, round one last bend to our left, we came upon our new home.

'Scacafell' was a small bungalow, once colour-washed in pale yellow distemper, now peeling and

Left: Scacafell, a holiday home.
Below: The view from the back garden, the drunken post being part of the boundary between garden and hayfield.

faded. It sat, like a one-storey doll's house, at the end of a short path behind a hedge wild with dog roses. The gate hung at an angle, open, inviting us weary travellers up through its front garden, mainly grass, with a row of trees to one side and a narrow path to the back of the house at the other. Daddy leaned the bicycle he'd collected from the station against a tall bush and pushed open the front door.

'Welcome!' he exclaimed, 'to our new home – well, for a bit anyway!' He put his arm round Mother and together they stepped out of the sunshine into the cool darkness of the cottage. Ruff's toes pattered on the linoleum floor, a cold welcome to hot tired paws and I blinked as I entered the low-ceilinged hallway. A figure appeared in a doorway to our left.

'Oh, there you are. Have a good journey?' Our new landlady was stocky with rich brown hair pulled back from her face. 'I just came along to make sure everything was ready. The kettle's on the stove in the kitchen,' she waved vaguely to her left, 'and I've brought a bit of bread and that, but I'll not stay. You'll want to get settled.' She pulled down the sleeves of her blouse before adding, 'Let me know if there's anything you want. You've got my number. The phone box is the other side of the station at the end of the road, opposite the shop.' And with that, she looked at us curiously, smiled, slipped past us and disappeared down the path.

'Oh, a cup of tea!' sighed Mother. 'Let's leave everything in the hall till we've eaten,' and she turned in the direction of the kitchen.

After a quick meal of eggs which had been left on a scrubbed table along with some Manx butter, yellow and strong ('definitely an acquired taste', Mother said), Ruff and I stood on top of two steps leading down from the kitchen door, and looked round, trying to take it all in. To my left under the kitchen window was a flat space of cracked flagstones; to the right pretty roses tumbled over a shed. As Mother had cooked lunch I had discovered that the little building *behind* the shed was an outside lavatory.

'Oh, lord!' Mother had exclaimed, before adding quickly 'Oh well, we're in the country now, and it makes this a holiday with a difference, doesn't it? We'll soon get used to it.'

Directly in front of the steps was a wide cinder path, which wound its way between untidy trees into what looked like a small field covered in rank grass. Was this the back garden? After the small town garden we'd left that morning, this was almost as unexpected as the outside toilet. But Ruff didn't stop to wonder. This was paradise to a dog with a sense of adventure! He plunged into the garden, his mischievous brown eyes sparkling as he charged around, following his nose, his sturdy white body frequently disappearing among humps of tall grass.

I followed, stumbling over uneven ground to arrive at the bottom of the garden beside the corrugated iron shed. Its door wouldn't open, so that must be left for another day. Beside it grew a row of spindly currant bushes. Berries hung like little strings of beads – rubies, pearls and jet – jewels just asking to be eaten, but disappointingly sour on the tongue.

'Come on, you two, bed time!' Mother's voice echoed down the garden. 'You can explore in the morning'.

I snuggled down in bed, happy to find that one of Daddy's cat drawings had been pinned to the pillow in welcome. Ruff snored loudly in the kitchen, and soon we slept, at peace because we were together again. Our holiday had begun.

Since it was the weekend, Daddy had been given leave for the first three days. So after breakfast, we retraced our steps to the railway station for another ride on the toy-like train to explore Ramsey, the only town in the north of the island. Here, a short walk from the station led to a square where there were a few shops, a small cinema and the start of Parliament Street.

'This is the main street,' explained Daddy, 'and all the main shops are along here. You should find everything you need. We'll take the ration books into Liptons or the Maypole, Pops, then you'll be on their books.'

I never knew why my diminutive mother was called 'Pops' by my six feet tall father (well, *six-foot-and-a-tea-leaf* is what he said he was). None of her family was tall, not even her father who gloried in the name of Theophilus Porter. Like him, all of his children had names which rolled richly of the tongue: Edith, Winifred, Clarice, Constance, Alice (my mother) and Theodora. Perhaps that's why I was given the simplest of names. Maybe because she was tiny, my father thought of Mother as his 'poppet'. I never knew either, why she called him Bill when his given name was Albert. But then many couples with 'a marriage made in heaven' (to quote Edith, my Aunty Det) have pet names for each other. This marriage was engineered in heaven by having Bill served in a Baker's shop by Mother was who was an apprentice there. But none of this concerned me. I just knew I was part of a large loving family.

Parliament Street ran straight through the town like its spine, with narrow streets running off it on either side. Seagulls called overhead and a vague smell of fish hung in the air. Following that smell down a side street we came upon the harbour. A few fishing boats rocked on the incoming tide flowing in from Ramsey's shallow bay some way to our right, beyond the main street and off a market square. A grey metal swing bridge stretched over the harbour and in the distance, beyond a row of tall boarding houses, we could just glimpse the sparkle of the sea. But my father said abruptly,

'We're not going over the bridge. We're going to find the beach and build some sand castles. I bet mine will be better than yours! Come on,' and he bustled us back into a newsagent's on the main street and while I chose a new bucket and spade, I heard him say quietly, 'Don't go into that part of town, Pops. Those houses are being used as an internment camp. There are about ten camps on the island now, maybe 14,000 civilian internees altogether. Those over the bridge – it's called the Mooragh – are mixed, mainly German and Finns, but keep away, dear, please.'

So the first couple of days passed in a flash as together we explored the town and spent a good deal of time playing on the quiet beach, splashing round in the sea and enjoying picnic meals. This was the perfect holiday and it was hard to remember there was a war on.

On Monday Daddy returned to his squadron. Before I was awake, he pedalled off along country roads to Jurby, five miles away, and returned in the evening. Mother and I were left to pass the day as we chose, walking the lanes and fields with Ruff, visiting Ramsey or just pottering round the garden, which in itself was something of an adventure. To me it was fun to be in a house without stairs and it didn't really matter that it was without electricity or hot water too. There was no hurry. We could wait for the kettle to boil on the fire or the little green oil stove. The sun shone most of the time, it was warm and we all knew that in less than two months our holiday would be over.

On Tuesday we visited the little shop at the top of our road, at crossroads nearly a ten minute walk from the house. Then Mother decided we might follow the main road, which appeared to run straight through the village.

'Oh yes,' the shop-keeper said, happy to impart information to a stranger, 'this bit's called the Sulby Straight.' She pointed her thumb to the left. 'It'll take you through Kirk Michael to Peel that way, or Ramsey and the north the other way, about four miles that is.' She nodded and snapped the drawer of the cash-till shut with a satisfactory little 'ting'.

The Straight's northern route led us from a church on the corner, past a large tree-lined field, then past a school and schoolhouse standing beside another church. Further on we came upon a cluster of cottages and a small flour mill. Opposite this was the Post Office, which drove Mother to say as we walked on, 'Oh, I must write to Aunty Det. Remind me to get stamps on the way back.' Det was her favourite sister and we knew she'd be longing to know how we were faring. More cottages appeared in the distance before the road took a sharp bend to the right as it crossed a river bridge, then dipped to a hotel on a corner before climbing a hill away towards Ramsey. But by now we were tired, so we turned back.

The bell on the post office door jangled and we found ourselves in what had once been the front room of a small terraced house. The room was sliced in half by a metal grill above a counter, which stretched across from one side wall to the other. Summoned by the bell, a little grey-haired post-mistress suddenly appeared from a room at the back. She stared at us inquisitively through the grill, but didn't speak.

'Two stamps, please,' said Mother brightly. 'Isn't it a lovely day?' The woman nodded, peered at us from beneath wiry brows and pushed the stamps forward. Then, head slightly tilted like a beady-eyed bird, she watched us as if waiting to be told where the stamps would be going. Mother smiled and as we left, the woman hurried back into her kitchen. What news she had for her neighbours, sitting there, drinking tea as they sifted through gossip. A stranger had called at the post office! A fly on the wall might have heard her say excitedly, 'she's only small and she's a little girl at her – must be the 'comeover' staying in the bungalow down Clenagh Road – you know, the one whose husband's at Jurby!'

Later that evening Daddy brought his flying boots to show us, zipped and furry inside, so deep that my legs were swallowed up by them. Then he let me help polish the buttons on his uniform. I followed his instructions carefully, slipping a piece of u-shaped card under each button to protect the fabric and then rubbing at the buttons until I could see my face in them. He really did look handsome in the uniform he wore so proudly.

He never said much about his squadron at Jurby, though training was becoming intense and a great deal of time was spent out of the classroom on bomb aiming exercises, flying out over the sea and further afield.

Ready to Fly 1942. Father centre, with the crew.

Exactly one week after our arrival in 'Scacafell', Thursday dawned again, the air, after the showers of the previous day, soft with the promise of summer's return. I slept on as the early morning ritual began. I knew how it went without seeing it...

Seven o'clock... 'Must go.' My father wheeled his bicycle down the path and his Pops pattered after him in her slippers. 'See you tea-time, darling,' he would say. A quick hug and a kiss and he set off, pedalling towards Jurby, turning to wave as he reached a distant bend in the road...

My mother stood on the quiet lane, waving and watching him go, as she had done each morning. Then she turned away to pluck a couple of wide-eyed pink roses which tumbled over the gate, and came back into the house.

The sun was bright and warm as we crossed from side to side of Parliament Street, shopping, collecting our rations for the weekend. Shops fascinated me, especially the big ones where the counter assistant dropped your money into a little metal canister and then sent it whizzing along a high overhead wire to the cashier. The cashier sat at her desk behind a window in a room set high against one wall of the shop. I always thought that would be a fine job, sitting waiting for money to come rushing at you as if by magic. The canister may or may not speed back to the counter with change. It all helped to make even the most boring shop fun.

'I wonder if we'll see the parrot?' I said as we went on to the end of the street.

I'd liked parrots ever since we'd once looked after one while a friend went on holiday. It was grey and it whistled very loudly –'like a paper-boy at work in the morning,' Daddy had said, and I'd tried to imagine it pushing newspapers through peoples' doors with its long-clawed feet. He never stayed again though. Mother got cross because he threw nutshells all over the floor. We'd seen the Ramsey parrot when Daddy first took us into town. He lived in a pub popular with local fishermen. Put out to air each morning, his cage hung in the doorway, from where he watched the world go by as he preened his dusty red and green feathers. He was quite a feature in the town, Daddy said, able to draw a crowd when he shouted out nursery rhymes. He was also very good at swearing and I longed for the day when I could report that a parrot had sworn at me!

On that Thursday, however, he wasn't there, and we were standing wondering whether to wait for him to appear or turn back, when a Land Rover drew up beside us. A smartly dressed woman stepped down from the driver's seat and moved towards Mother.

'Excuse me,' she said gently, 'could you spare me a minute,' she hesitated and looked towards me, 'in private?' At a wondering nod from Mother, I took a step across the pavement to look in a shop window in the corner next to the pub. What did this strange woman want? I couldn't remember seeing her before. I gazed down into the window of a cobbler's shop, its window so large that it nearly reached the pavement, its contents destined to be remembered forever. Grouped round a hammer beside a shoemaker's last in the middle of the display, was a brown boot, a pair of Wellingtons, two floral slippers and, unexpectedly, a red, high heeled shoe perched on its own on a glass stand. Time stood still. Then I felt the woman tap my shoulder. I turned, and as I did so it was as if I was suddenly lifted from my innocent, comfortable, seven-year-old existence where I took everything for granted, to one where I would see things as they really were.

The adult world was about to come into focus.

Chapter 3

The woman didn't speak as she helped me into the high front seat of the vehicle to sit beside Mother, who sat silent, just staring ahead. Then we were driven away from the pub, past the fine white police station on the opposite corner, along the streets and up a road, which gradually climbed away from the town. Still nothing was said as we entered a house, to arrive in a kitchen. A bottle clinked against a tall glass as the woman poured a drink, took a comic from somewhere, opened the back door and ushered me into the garden. 'There you are, my dear,' she said indicating a small wooden chair beside some shrubs and a flowerbed. 'You sit there and read the comic. I hope you like lemonade. You drink it up while I go and talk to your mother,' and smiling brightly, she disappeared back into the house.

Sitting in the quiet garden, I suddenly felt cold. Something was wrong. The stranger was too kind, and why had Mother not spoken? It was as if she hadn't even known I was there. Mickey Mouse waved at me from the front of the comic, but I didn't want to read and it slipped from my knee. I didn't want to drink either. I sat frozen in the sunshine, twisting Sylvia's necklace at my throat and trying not to feel sick.

Sylvia and I had exchanged presents at Christmas. In exchange for a shimmering bracelet of red beads, which Sylvia had chosen from my own collection, she'd given me this necklace. It was made of plastic buttons, shaped like lacy flowers, six blue ones alternating with six smaller pink ones, each joined together by a small round-headed paper fastener. Tied at each end with blue cord, it was fastened round my neck. 'Now we'll always remember each other,' Sylvia had said.

The minutes ticked by and the butterflies in my stomach seemed to become dragonflies, whirring, pressing painfully against me, inside. I twisted the necklace tighter and it snapped, collapsing into my hand. Tears pricked my eyes. What was happening? What was wrong? It was as if the sun had suddenly lost its warmth, and everything was so quiet. Only a faint breeze whispered in the leaves beside me. Then the woman appeared again.

'Come along, dear,' she said, holding out her hand. 'I'm going to take you and your mother home.' I looked at the broken necklace, wordlessly.

'Oh dear,' said the woman and she bent to touch it. 'It's broken. Never mind, I'm sure it will mend.'

But not everything 'mends' so easily.

Nothing was said on the journey home, but I was to find that my stricken mother had suddenly become a widow. My father, aged 34, Leading Aircraftsman Snelson, RAF No.1439634 – I'd learned his number with pride and knew it so well – had been killed. At 8.45 am, one year and two days after he joined up and less than two hours since he'd waved a cheery goodbye, he and his crew in a twin-engined Blenheim bomber were involved in a mid-air collision with a second Blenheim. The planes were carrying out a training exercise, which involved them making mock attacks against each other for the benefit of a camera gun. Pilot error caused the loss of both crews. It happened only about twelve miles away, on the west coast of the island, south east of Peel. Both aircraft crashed near a farm on a hillside at Knockaloe, a place which for many years was just a name to us.

It seemed that they had been following the coastline when the sun blinded one of the pilots... maybe? Wingtips touched, perhaps, or...what? If Pops was ever told exactly how she had lost her Bill, she never ever said so. From my own research, many decades later, I was to learn that eyewitnesses reported that there had appeared to be contact between the aircraft. As they flew close together in a southerly direction, the rear plane banked sharply as it passed my father's Blenheim, then it dived to the right, struck the ground and burst into flames. His plane, the leading aircraft, had sent out smoke before suffering the same fate in an adjoining field. Pieces of wreckage were scattered over the area, but nobody was able to rescue the crews from the burning aircraft. All Mother knew that morning was that she had lost her husband. On that day she wrote in her diary 'My Darling killed. End of a wonderful life.' The rest of the pages remained blank forever.

The following days were a blur. By Saturday we had been joined by two of my aunts, Bertha and Det, both of whom had dropped everything to travel to the island to do what they could to help their sister. On the first evening, Det, quite overcome with grief, sank down on the arm of a chair in the front room, clutching Daddy's photograph in one hand and me in the other.

'Oh, look at him,' she moaned, waving the picture under my nose. 'Look. To think we'll never, ever see him again, never.' Tears poured down her cheeks. I gazed at her, feeling hollow inside, and unable to cry. Nobody had really explained to me what all this trouble was about. The truth was beginning to dawn on me, but it was all so far from reality that it was beyond my comprehension. I felt as if I'd stretched out, as I often did, to hug my arms round my father, to feel the security of his strong and solid body, only to find that he'd suddenly melted away and I was left with nothing to hold but myself.

'Oh, be quiet, Det!' said Mother fiercely. 'We can't sit here moaning. I'm not the first and I won't be the last. I've got to think what to do.'

'Well, it's obvious what you must do,' replied Bertha in her best, bossy Bertha voice. 'You must come back with us. You can't stay here now.'

'No, of course you can't,' echoed Edith. 'You'll be all on your own. You don't know anyone here. Of course you'll come back with us after the funeral,' and at that thought, she dissolved again.

'No!' Mother stood up, fighting back her own tears. 'No, I'm going to stay. I promised Bill. He'd want us here until the war's over because we'll be safer here, so we stay for the duration. I shall arrange to go on renting this place.'

'But you can't stay here! It's, it's …' Words failed Bertha as she looked round the little sitting room. 'It's in the middle of nowhere. It hasn't got electricity or hot water – it hasn't even got a bathroom!' Her voice shook with indignation. 'You can't live in a place like this! However would you manage?'

'I don't know, but I will!' Mother's tiny frame stood resolute. 'I know you mean well, but I promised Bill. And this place will do until I can find somewhere better.' There was silence as the sisters faced each other. I looked from one to the other. I had never seen Mother stand so straight or look so determined. The argument had swirled round me as I leaned against Auntie Det, feeling cold and white and lost. I felt so tired. I just wanted to close my eyes for a long time, and then wake up to find that everything was all right again and Daddy was there with drawings of his special cats in his hand.

There were no more tears, at least not when I was around. In time I came to understand that Mother was a stoic, firmly believing – and stating – that anyone's problem, even grief, was his own private affair. That was how it was then. We must just get on with it. Tomorrow was another day. The only official acknowledgment of my father's death, apart from reams of forms to fill in, was a kind letter from his superior officer at Jurby and a cold, impersonal mass-printed card with my mother's name typed across the bottom. Purported to come from the Palace, complete with duplication of the King's signature, it offered sympathy for 'a life so nobly given'. Thousands must have been sent out automatically and it felt as if nobody really cared. At the beginning of the next century the results of psychological studies would show that a great consequence of two world wars was the emotional damage which had been caused to those caught up in them. The lives of two generations were reshaped, so that all too often both adults and children found it difficult to show their feelings or to say good-bye. I can vouch for that.

But it was still only 1942 and we had our lives to live.

There were a few visitors to the little bungalow. One RAF officer arrived from the station to offer advice. Another appeared with Daddy's bicycle, and our landlady came and agreed to the signing of a long rental agreement. But on the day after Mother had announced her decision, I was wandering aimlessly round the front garden, with Ruff at my heels, when I heard the sound of a heavy lorry. Curious, because traffic was rare, I hung over the front gate and was just in time to see a long trailer trundling past in the direction of the aerodrome. On board were great chunks of twisted metal, bits of fuselage, the tail fins of what I knew, with a sudden deadly certainty, was all that remained of the crashed aircraft. But I didn't tell Mother what I'd seen. I didn't want to upset her. Already I remembered the words once whispered in my ear, 'Look after Mother for me'. I knew that I would try.

And all the while she and her sisters did what they could, for my sake, to establish some routine in our lives, lives which had suddenly been turned upside down. Mother refused to go to the funeral, helpfully organised by Wing-Commander Alford, the Station Commander. It was held in the bleak wind-swept church of St Patrick overlooking the sea at Jurby. There Bill still rests, with his 20 year old Polish pilot and members of other crews who had met the same fate earlier in the year, and some who would join them later. Mother, a stranger in a strange place, couldn't face the funeral and she believed it was no event for a child. As an adult, I was to wonder if she was right.

At last my aunts had to return to their families, but

they travelled back across the Irish Sea with us under their collective wing. For Mother there was still much to be done in England, not least the termination of the lease on the Cheshire house, which had been the family home and to which we briefly returned. Our faithful neighbour was there to pray over us and to help with arrangements for the sale or storage of furniture and fittings – the latter task one which I believe Mother felt was the more valuable of the two.

'We've got to sort out all the things we want to take with us,' Mother said to me. 'So go upstairs and put yours together so they can be sent on.' Where should I start? I treasured everything I had. Then she turned to the unenviable job herself, packing, organising, notifying officials, doing all that had to be done before we could return to the island to wait out the war. And feeling lost, I drifted through the muddled days.

'Look,' Mrs Booth said one morning, 'you can't carry all that with you. Put aside the things you want me to pack and I'll send them on to you,' a suggestion gratefully, if unwisely, accepted. So a permit was obtained from the Censorship Department in Liverpool for items to be sent to the island, and boxes were packed in such a way that Customs Officers could inspect our belongings if they wanted to.

'So much red tape,' Mother sighed as she coped with it all, and I looked on and wondered why I couldn't see any. Then as it began to come to an end Mother came wearily into the kitchen carrying a large cardboard box, which she set down by the hearth. Our cats, Ni**er, tortoiseshell Topsy and her kitten Tico, who had been watching all that was going on from their chair by the fire, peered at it suspiciously.

'This will have to do for the cats,' she said. Mrs Booth looked at it doubtfully.

'They'll never all fit in there,' she said softly. 'Look, shall I keep Ni**er here with me? He's old now and we're used to each other.' She tickled him behind one ear and he stretched out a paw. Sadly we gazed at the cats. Another decision to be made. 'I suppose you're right', Mother agreed at last. 'We'll just take Topsy and Tico then.'

The long journey back to the island, this time quite without any anticipation or excitement, was tiring but uneventful, and at last Mother and I, a box full of cat and various cases and parcels, were deposited once more beneath the veranda on Sulby Glen's station platform. The train trundled off to its shed while Fred, the stocky little station-master, looked at us, blue eyes kind in his weather-worn face.

'Back again then,' he said, smiling. 'Back again. Aye, aye,' and pushing his cap to the back of his head, he wandered off up the platform, the warm aromatic smell of his pipe smoke drifting after him. News travels fast in the country and everyone in the village would know our story, but although they were interested, inquisitive even, they would not be over-inclined to offer help. After all, we were 'comeovers' not Manx born. We would find that although an outsider is treated kindly, it takes Ellan Vannin many years to accept him. But in 1942 all we knew was that we felt safe on the island and we would stay for as long as was necessary.

It was some time before it dawned on me that living on an island in wartime meant that we could no longer visit the family as we used to do. I couldn't go to Auntie Con's and have tea with my cousins David and Hilton, who showed me how to smack the bottom of a tomato sauce bottle to make it splodge its delicious contents on to egg and chips. I'd miss dancing round in cousin Dorothy's pretty dresses at Aunt Bertha's or sitting while she brushed and curled my hair. How long would it be before I could enjoy again the luxury of two home-made puddings at once – jam tart nestling in rice pudding – as I remembered from when we went to dinner at Auntie Det's and Uncle Eddie's?

Their house was bereft of toys, for they had no children, but I loved going there. I was allowed to scrabble through kitchen drawers for 'treasure'. I sat at Auntie's dressing table among the perfumes and lipsticks, or gazed in wonder at the frothy confections of sequins and tulle which hung in her wardrobe. Det and Eddie's hobby was ballroom dancing and several shining trophies on their sideboard showed how successful they were.

After tea, Uncle Eddie, as warm and cuddly as a teddy bear, would lean back in his armchair and invite me to sit on his knee while he told me a story. Half way through he'd close his eyes and snore gently... Although I knew what would happen next, I'd try to get down. But his arms would tighten round me and the more I struggled, the tighter they became until as

I began to panic, Auntie Det would say 'Wake up Uncle,' and he'd open one eye.

'Dear me, did I go to sleep?' Then he'd laugh and add, 'Well, the cat got the mouse that time, didn't it?'

I was too old for cat and mouse the next time we met.

With her cousins two years earlier — from left: Hilton, David, the author and their friend Jim.

Chapter 4

*I*t would be almost impossible to record our new life on Ellan Vannin chronologically. Memory doesn't work like that. Some dates flash like a spark to highlight an event or a turning point, to act as a marker in the years which, tumbling together, form the memories which make up 'childhood', but they don't recall it all. A certain date could be the first day at school, the day war ended, an illness recognised or a competition won. But who can remember exactly how, or when they first came to know the eccentric old woman on her bicycle, or first saw a place which was to spell happiness? How long did it take for Mother and me to fall into the Manx 'traa-dy looar' way of life, to learn not to rush but to say 'time enough' when something must be done? It's impossible to say. Then too, since we had no transport and very little money, it was many years before we were able to see the island's historical treasures and how much unspoilt physical beauty it offers. So I must begin with our new centre of security, the village and the house which was destined to become 'home', and move on from there as memory dictates.

Sulby village, part of the largest parish of Lezayre in the north of the island, was and is scattered, but it has everything that one would expect. Its name stems from the Scandinavian Solabyr, meaning Sola's farm – many Manx place names are of Celtic or Scandinavian origin. It lies at the foot of a glen carved out by the Sulby River, at 10½ miles the longest on the island. In time we would find the Glen to be beautiful, the hillsides a soft green with scattered farms, or covered with bracken, heather and gorse, the natural home for sheep and goats. From Tholt-e-Will at the top, the narrow metalled road widens as it drops down beside the river so that the hills appear higher than they are.

A modern view of Sulby Glen, going towards Tholt-Y-Will.

Then it joins the main Peel to Ramsey road on the Straight, thereby forming a crossroads with our Clenagh Road. Here was the shop and the Methodist Church; one of Sulby's two pubs, conveniently placed at either end of the village, and two railway stations, 'ours' Sulby Glen, and Sulby Bridge a short distance to the north. The school and its schoolhouse sat next to St Stephen's Church a few hundred yards north of the crossroads. A little further on from the school were the Post Office we'd already visited and the Kella Flour Mill.

This was our new village as we first saw it, but we were soon to find that there was more to it than that. If we turned left before going up the Glen for example, and walked along a short, dappled lane we came upon a splendid dog-walking area and what was later to become a playground for me, and the friends I was yet to make. This was the Claddagh, (water meadow land) reached by crossing a bridge over the river, an area which in the future would become popular with campers.

'Scacafell' as a holiday home had been fun, but we looked at it differently when it became a more permanent dwelling. Its charm must have faded very rapidly for Mother, who now faced rebuilding her life far away from family, friends and most recognised forms of modern urban living. This small, four-roomed bungalow with a green front door, which proved difficult to shut in wet weather, crouched at the end of a concrete path with a gate which agreed to open only if it was lifted slightly. Four doors led off the windowless hallway wide enough, we later discovered, to accommodate with ease a bookcase and a bicycle. To the right were two bedrooms, each with a deep sashed window and a small iron fireplace. My parents had taken the back room, while I had the front room which not only had a double bed, like the back room, but also a single bed beneath the window.

'We'll stay in the bedrooms we had,' Mother decided, and leaning her forehead against the cold glass of the back window, she peered out, without really seeing the garden shed, and the riot of pink roses which smothered half its walls and corrugated iron roof. There must have been a pact among the doors of our new home, for this shed, too, had a door definitely averse to closing and its rusty bolt seemed to be for decoration only.

It was not until the onset of winter that we began to notice that the bedroom in which we now stood had a decidedly musty smell – you never really get to know the secrets of any house until you've lived in it for a while. As time went on, we also discovered that the walls in this room wept all the year round, were faintly damp to the touch in summer and sometimes openly ran with water as the year dipped down to Christmas. Newly distempered, they soon became discoloured and any wallpaper showed quite clearly that it preferred to hang in graceful loops. But it was, after all, just a country cottage, built at a time when a damp course wasn't something that the builder had thought about.

The first door on the left of the hall opened into 'the front room' small but pleasant enough and complete with a grate, whose idiosyncrasies we'd come to know well as autumn drew on. The window here looked out into the front garden, and opposite this stood the door into the kitchen, a smaller room complete with a heavy black range with two ovens to the left of the fireplace, one above the other. The smaller top one with its hinged, drop down door, was never closed or used for cooking, but it became, as the years went on, the favourite sleeping place for various cats who were to join the family.

Off the kitchen to the right was a minute scullery, an extension of the hall and closed off from it by an unpainted wooden door with a latch. Here were some shelves above a small table, a deep stone sink with a cold-water tap and beside that, to the left, a little window at waist level. This dark little place became not only 'wash-room' but also a larder of sorts. In summer bottles of milk and dishes of margarine or perishable food stood on the table in bowls of cold water – the only refrigerator we had. Beside them, a small free-standing wooden cupboard with a door of fine wire mesh kept other foods out of the reach of flies.

The back door led directly out of the kitchen into the large garden, along the left side of which, and separated by chicken wire, ran a neighbour's hayfield.

This was 'Scacafell', our new home. Its name, we were told, was the Manx equivalent of the Scandinavian 'skogar fell' meaning a wooded hill – Sky Hill to the north, near Ramsey, which we could see from the garden.

It was all very different from most houses on the

island, and the tall urban terraced house we had left behind with its long staircase and all mod cons. Now we had no hot water system, gas or electricity and neither bathroom nor indoor toilet. Everything formerly taken for granted was missing. The holiday home had become a house full of grim realities. And to we city dwellers there was nothing more grim than the horrors of an outside lavatory.

This was of a universal design known for centuries. Set within a small, windowless wooden shed a short distance from the back door, and beneath trees which moaned on windy nights, it had a hinged wooden seat and a hole, beneath which rested a bucket. It was not a 'double-seater', as were some in the country, so one couldn't pass the time in gossip with a friend. On a handy nail to the right regulation squares of newspaper hung on a string, and I soon learned to soften the paper by crumpling it well before use – after reading it first, of course. I have never been able to resist the printed word. Perhaps that's a legacy from this newsworthy toilet paper, for the real thing was in short supply during the war. Even when it became available it was often in the form of thin sheets interleaved in a flat square box, under the brand name Izal, and it still needed crumpling to be comfortable in use.

Our 'convenience' was bad enough during the day, but it was worse at night. Wrapped in a coat and clutching a torch, we hurried into this tiny building, lifted the lid, wondered if rats were lurking beneath and then sat shivering for as short a time as possible. It was unpleasant, cold and draughty, especially since the latched door stopped short of the ground by about three inches. And that was not all. The thing had to be emptied. There were no 'night soil operatives' here. At first, when Mother took on this role, I used to hover and try to help, but by the time I was nine or ten it fell my lot to empty the bucket regularly. It was fortunate that we had a large, rambling field for a back garden, for over the years I had to dig a great many deep holes round the edge of it. Then in went the contents of the bucket, followed by a liberal handful of lime. Wash out the bucket with Izal or Jeyes Fluid, pour that in the shed too, then it was ready for the whole sequence to begin again. It was no wonder that the 'po' under the bed became a very necessary and permanent feature of life, especially in winter.

Lack of a family bathroom, once taken for granted, meant other difficulties. A cold-water tap in a little scullery doesn't lend itself to fastidious personal hygiene, especially in the early morning when the fire sulks and refuses to heat the kettle – although I must admit that a face washed in icy water before breakfast will waken any child most efficiently. At first a bath took the form of a laborious 'bit at a time' wash-down by the sink, but Mother soon changed that.

We'd only been there a few months when I arrived home from school to hear her announce proudly, 'Look what I got in Ramsey.' She pointed to the back of the kitchen door where hung, in time-honoured fashion, a small tin bath. 'Second hand, of course, but I've given it a damn good clean, so it'll be fine.' Thereafter we bathed regularly in front of the kitchen fire, our bodies burning nearest the heat, while a draught from the back door brought up goose pimples everywhere else. That was until we hit on the idea of enclosing the bathing space with a wooden clothes-horse (airer) draped with towels or a sheet. We were then not only warmer, but we had some modicum of privacy. But of course our bodies were not all that had to be washed.

'I can't get these dishes clean,' I moaned. 'They're all greasy.'

'Well use the soap saver again,' said Mother crossly. 'Swish it hard.' She was on her hands and knees raking out ash from beneath the kitchen grate. 'Or would you rather do this?' She turned and pushed hair off her face with a grimy hand.

'There's not much soap.' I peered at the odds and ends of hard green soap in their little wire cage at the end of the metal handle I was holding.

'There's not much of anything!' was the retort, 'if you can't get them clean, throw in some soda crystals or heat another kettle on the stove. Use your brain!' and Mother staggered out into the garden with a bucket full of ash and cinders. So I swished violently and the soap saver clattered against the washing up bowl until at last a cloud of bubbles appeared. Then, with a lot of rubbing from the dishcloth, the plates finally lost their greasy look. If only someone had invented washing up liquid earlier!

Washing anything in Scacafell was hard work, especially clothes and bedding. For this we found a grey metal dolly tub in the shed and a big mangle with wooden rollers. Monday, weather permitting, was generally washday – there was routine in everything we did. Routine gave a semblance of order in an uncertain wartime life and without it we would never have got through all the chores. So washing was soaked in the tub on Sunday night to 'loosen the dirt' ready for the next morning. Then kettles of hot water with soap or soda crystals, or when available, precious Rinso washing powder, were added. Everything was then swished around with a dolly (which resembled a small four-legged stool with a long central handle) or scrubbed against the corrugated surface of a metal washboard, thoughtfully left by someone in our dolly tub. The trick was to take away dirty marks without allowing the scrubbing brush to take away the fabric, but struggle one must, for cleanliness was next to godliness. After a rinsing, when a little blue dolly bag was sometimes added to the water to whiten the sheets (something I could never understand) the washing had to be wrung out – not too difficult by hand with small items, but impossible with bed linen.

'Hold that sheet off the ground while I mangle,' Mother would order – or sometimes it might be me who had to keep fingers away from the heavy rollers as we pushed reluctant sheets between them until flattened. At last, pegged out over the washing line, which stretched from a nail by the back door to a tree on the back path, and held aloft by a wooden clothes prop, our laundry danced until dry in the ever-present winds – unless it rained. Then, 'Drat this washing!' and Mother, dodging the drips, would heave a long wooden clothes rack up towards the kitchen ceiling. There various items festooned the kitchen until dry. It was always a full day's work. But Mother had known hard work in the bakery where she worked before marriage and she had been brought up never to fail when presented with a challenge.

* * *

So in 1942, having arrived back in Scacafell, and with all this still ahead, Mother buttered both cats' paws so that they wouldn't stray and let them out of the kitchen door. Trusting that Ruff would look after them, she watched them wander off down the cinder path, and then turned to me standing uncertainly in the funny little kitchen.

'Tea and bed,' she announced with assumed brightness, 'and then tomorrow we'll sort ourselves out. Mrs Booth will send on your toys, so you'll soon have those to play with, and we'll have a lot to do, won't we – lots of things we haven't done before, I expect. Now don't worry, we'll be all right here, we'll be safe, and that's what Daddy wanted. Now, where's the teapot?'

She was right, of course. We were safe. After a while it was easy to forget that there was a war on, even though training aircraft droned overhead so frequently. They practised dropping flares and smoke bombs over Jurby beach and sometimes we heard of more crashes involving aircraft from Jurby, or Andreas where Spitfires were based for a while; or of planes lost en route from somewhere else. But we knew all about these accidents. We couldn't be hurt again. So after a while we didn't notice the planes, because we knew that they posed no threat to us. There was no blitz, no air-raids signalled by the heart-stopping 'warbling' of the warning siren. From Sulby we couldn't see a glow in the sky, which in England meant that thousands of people were suffering the nightly demolition of their homes and businesses. No portly silver barrage balloons hovered overhead and it wasn't really necessary to have patterns of tape or paper criss-crossing the windows to minimise the danger of flying glass after a bomb blast. There may have been the occasional thump as a bomb was jettisoned from a plane on its way home, but I can't say that I recall it.

We continued to use the blackout blinds of stiff black linen that Mother had brought from Cheshire – dismal rollers with a tendency to shoot up of their own volition suddenly and unexpectedly. But we never actually heard the 'Put that light out!' order so often barked in England. We found that there were no street lights in the countryside anyway, and it was some time before we developed eyes like our cats' so that we could walk confidently through the darkness. At night we never went anywhere without a torch, always shaded by a careful hand. Only once did I forget, and that was when, some time later, I was walking home alone.

It was November, cold, but for once the 'invigorating' Manx wind was still and the road was filled with silence. Halfway home and passing fields, I heard, from behind the hedge, a distinct cough, a harsh grating noise – too loud to be human, I thought in my terror. It was repeated, and I can honestly say that I never covered the five hundred yards to our gate at such speed again. I had thought I was becoming a country girl, but didn't know a sheep's cough when I heard one!

Food on the island was rationed, but the Manx were not dependent on rations alone. There were always more vegetables, eggs, butter, even chickens to be had if you knew the right person and had money to spare. Here, unfortunately, we were unlucky. It was a long time before we knew people well enough to be given favours and as for money, that was something we definitely did not have. My mother's weekly war pension was £1 14s 6d – £1.5s with 9s 6d extra for me (£1.72½p). If it hadn't been for occasional financial support from the Aunts, especially dear Auntie Det who slipped a ten-shilling note in her letters when she could, there were many times when we just could not have survived, even though Mother worked. So, along with many others, we scrimped and saved, tried most of the wartime recipes suggested on government pamphlets, turned sugar bags inside out to get the last grain and became accustomed to making a little go a long way.

The Islanders, being dependent to a large extent on shipping for commodities, had known how war would affect them. The blitz on the Liverpool docks in September 1940, to which my father had been sent as a fire-fighter, had demonstrated that. When the Coburg Dock was bombed on 27th September that year, 35 tons of cargo destined for Ramsey were lost, and a month later a Manx Steam Packet depot on No 5 Dock received a direct hit. In December 1941, six months before we travelled, the steamer Victoria, sailing to Douglas, was mined 8 miles from Liverpool, but fortunately was able to be towed back to safety with no loss of life. Earlier in the previous year, too, the Island had been looked toward for another reason.

Geographically set apart as it was, and far enough away from centres of military importance – the RAF stations at Jurby and Andreas were training stations – the Isle of Man was an ideal area for evacuees and the internment of those considered dangerous to national security. In May 1940 the Manx newspapers had announced that, not for the first time, internment camps were to be created on the Island. During the First World War there had been a 'village' of wooden huts near Peel on the west coast, where 23,000 aliens had been kept. Now several camps were once again created in various parts of the island, but this time houses were requisitioned by the government who paid rent for the property. Some internees were refugees, others 'enemy aliens', but many were found to pose no risk and were released, especially the old and the sick. Some even began to work on farms, replacing local men who had left the island to join the forces when war was declared. We were neither internees nor refugees – evacuees perhaps – but whatever our status, we were glad to have the island as our new home, even if we didn't know for how long that would be.

Chapter 5

I was awakened by the dull sound of banging and scraping. I listened for a minute then padded through to the kitchen where I found Mother once again on her hands and knees in front of the grate.

'I really must remember to bank up the fire at night,' she said, bending forward to blow into a little pile of wood and coals. 'I can't be bothered with this palaver every morning. At least if it's banked up there'll be a flicker of heat left to get it going.' I perched on the edge of the table to watch. A thin wisp of smoke began to curl up the chimney. She blew again. The wisp grew stronger and then suddenly it puffed back into her face.

'Oh, blast the thing!' she exclaimed, and grabbing the nearby shovel, she stood it upright on the edge of the grate, the handle leaning up against the front of the surround. 'Hand me that paper,' and she stretched out for a sheet of newspaper on the table. It was obviously now destined for something greater than being torn into squares to hang in the lavatory. She spread the newspaper across the shovel and holding it either side of the fireplace, she bent and blew several times beneath it. A little roaring sound indicated that the sticks had taken light.

'That'll do it.' Mother sat back on her heels. We watched as the paper across the hot shovel gradually began to change colour from white to pale yellow, and then to toast brown. Then little red-gold holes sparkled across the newsprint.

'That's it!' Mother exclaimed triumphantly and she quickly snatched the shovel away and bundled the now flaming paper up the chimney. 'An old trick, but don't try it!' she said. Other 'tricks', which she employed in those fire-lighting days, included lumps of fat strategically placed among the sticks and coal as she set them or, when she was really desperate, paraffin. She would hurl the oil on to the coals, toss in a lighted match, and stand back hoping for the best. But on this morning, as the flaming paper roared up the chimney, she added, 'And I think we'd better get these chimneys swept before winter.'

A sweep did come eventually, complete with long black sweep's brushes which he screwed together with soot engrained hands, and a shovel to scoop his success into a container which look like an over-grown bucket. As he laid an old sheet across the floor in the front room, Mother remarked, 'This one really need sweeping. The smoke blows back worse than in the kitchen.'

'That'll be the wind,' came the reply. 'Don't matter how clean 'tis, if the wind's in the wrong direction, smoke'll blow back.' The sweep pushed back his cap and bent to his work. 'No, no, nothin' you can do about that, I'm afraid.' And there wasn't. But by watching the winds, we learned when to use wood instead of smoky coal and to remember that little black specks, which sometimes floated before our eyes, were merely soot and not the onset of some fearful visual disturbance. The sweep only came once. After that Mother regularly did what our neighbours appeared to do – thrust a piece of lighted gorse up the chimney, then, with fingers crossed, run out into the garden to make sure the whole roof hadn't gone up in flames!

We wouldn't have had all this trouble, of course, if the house had been wired for electricity. But we depended on the fire or paraffin for heat, light and cooking, so that gradually Mother's shiny pans became blackened with smoke. As that first summer faded and the dark nights came in, it was a long time before we stopped putting up a hand to the wall to switch on the light. Instead, we had to adjust to lamp lit evenings and the warm, oily smell that were part of them. We learned that if we wanted to avoid a thin tendril of smoke drifting from an oil lamp's blackening glass chimney, we must remember to keep the wick trimmed and not turn it up too high. We tried a Tilley lamp once, which had a mantle instead of a wick, but we had to keep pumping it up and it made a popping noise, so we soon gave that up. The Aladdin Lamp, also sporting a fragile mantle and a square black base which held the oil, was the best form of lighting, especially when Mother fixed a little shelf high on the front room wall for it to stand on. Shadows were banished, but the low ceiling began to discolour – until she solved that by nailing a biscuit tin lid to the ceiling above it. Necessity is the mother of invention!

It was Sunday, most of our things had been unpacked and we decided that we'd take Ruff for a walk and explore a little. It was cloudy and a chill breeze blew, but we were soon to discover that on this island a breeze, if not the strong prevailing southwest wind, blows most days. Ellan Vannin is not the place for complicated hairstyles. Even in these first weeks Mother tried to make our weekends busy, for somehow when you're on your own these can be the loneliest days. So she always found something we must do – tidying cupboards and drawers, cleaning out the sheds, scouring the countryside for wood or working in the untidy field that passed for our garden.

As each season dictated, we cut back the grass with a small curved sickle – a long two-handled scythe was as big as Mother – sheared off wayward branches, sawed up wood for the fire. Then, too, there were always holes to be patched up in the hedges, in a vain attempt to keep Ruff within our boundaries, for he was a dog who loved the great outdoors. He enjoyed life to the full and hedges presented an irresistible challenge. Whether he burrowed for rats, buried a bone, or just fought his way through for the hell of it, a hedge was

always something to be scrambled through. Eventually the base of our hawthorn and dog-rose boundary became a patchwork of old wood, chicken wire and odd bits of tin; but still he would wriggle his way out of the garden to disappear over the fields for hours or to sit unconcerned in the middle of the road. Then, what little traffic there was, generally drove carefully round him. It was for his benefit that Sunday walks became a regular feature.

This was the first time since the crash that we had deliberately set out to discover where our lane went.

With the dog bounding ahead, we turned left out of the gate and began to walk up the road away from the direction of the station and the shop. This was the way to the aerodrome, but that was five miles away and instinctively we knew that neither of us would state this fact nor walk that far just yet.

The road had no pavement, it was just wide enough for two vehicles to pass and it was deserted. All we could hear was the swish of wind in the trees and curlews calling over marshy fields to our right. The hedges were untidy, but bright with nodding flowers of wild fuchsia and the gossamer heads of old man's beard. Tall cow parsley and deep grass grew along the sides of the road and sometimes only Ruff's tail told us where he was, as he snuffled excitedly among the strange country smells.

We passed one or two houses and then after a few minutes came across a Manx 'tholtan', the roofless, crumbling ruins of a long-gone cottage. We discovered later that these, by tradition, were never pulled down but left as a shelter for the 'little people' and that this particular tholtan was known by the curious name of 'the smelters', though we never knew why or what it meant. The ruin had an eerie air, hiding as it did behind dark elder bushes overgrown by ivy and nettles and a green tangle of weeds, and eventually I learned to call Elder by its Manx name, Tramman. Believed to be a great antidote to witchcraft, it was often planted near cottages. But even before I knew this, the smelters looked creepy and I wouldn't have been surprised to see a bony finger beckoning or hear a cackle of laughter in the wind.

'Well, at least our garden isn't as bad as that,' observed Mother mildly. 'I wonder who lived there,' but we never knew.

As we walked on, the houses became fewer, and here and there a field gate in the tangled hedges allowed us to peer into fields. Sheep nibbled in one or two, but in others the ground was marshy, for patches of soft white cotton grass swayed in the wind. Then, after a couple of miles we came upon a small copse of pine trees to our right. It looked completely out of place, sitting beside the road as if it had been dropped there by accident. These tall pines, which we named 'the plantation', moaned even on the stillest day, and I always felt that if I stepped beneath the shadowy branches, I'd be lost forever.

'I think it's time we turned back,' Mother remarked. 'We can go further next time.' As we walked back, we could see in the distance, the smoky blue summit of Snaefell. This means 'snow mountain' in Scandinavian, although it rarely lives up to its name. At 2,034ft, it is the island's highest mountain, with the greens and browns of other hills stretching out on either side of it. Then half way home we noticed two figures in front of us. They were both small and muffled in old coats. The man carried a couple of rusty looking buckets while the other, a woman, pushed a large, battered coach-built pram. By the time we came abreast of them, they'd heaved open a field gate and the woman was dragging the pram over some bumpy ruts of dried mud. She looked up briefly and smiled. A blanket flopped over the side, but since the hood was up, I was unable to see what was inside. The man turned. 'Good day,' he said, a cheery grin appearing above an unshaven chin. 'Taking the air?'

'Yes,' answered Mother. 'You look as if you're off to do some work.'

'Oh, us,' the man replied. 'Oh Julia and me, we're off peaing.' He waved the buckets in the air. 'Should be able to fill these between us.' He grinned again, pulled his cap further on his head and the couple moved on up the field. Rather startled by his words, we stood by the gate, which they hadn't bothered to close.

'Well,' said Mother at last, 'what a funny pair! I wonder if they're all like that round here?' In fact, we were to meet nobody in the village who turned out to be as generous or as kind as this couple and we got to know them very well. Perhaps Mother felt compassion for them, as possibly they did for her, although clearly their lot was much worse than ours. But before that we came across someone else, someone who had a profound effect on both of us, and we never even knew her name.

Later that week even I could clearly see that Mother was upset and worried, and this was not surprising. She'd left a life she knew in England and we were alone. We didn't know our neighbours and at that time there were no counselling agencies to offer advice to war widows. Apart from having a roof over our heads and rented furniture, we had nothing. She became unusually tearful and angry when she couldn't find a needle and cotton, which had somehow got lost in the packing.

'I've got to have it now,' she snapped, when I made some vague remark about it turning up eventually. 'We'll have to go and get some more.'

So on the following morning we trotted down Ramsey's Parliament Street and into a wide-windowed shop, which seemed to be the centre of the town's lingerie and embroidery trade. It was a business run by two ladies, polite and soft-spoken, and while one served Mother I gazed at a beautiful embroidered cloth draped across a stand on the counter. It was edged with flowers and leaves and in the middle there was a picture of what looked like three legs joined together in the middle like spokes in a wheel. Each leg bore a spur on the ankle. I'd seen the design before, but couldn't remember where. The legs were bright red, but the words around them, beautifully stitched in brown, I couldn't read, let alone understand.

'That's the Manx emblem,' said a quiet voice, and the second of the two ladies smiled at me across the counter. 'It's on our flag, and the words – well, they're in Latin. 'Quocunque jeceris stabit'. They mean 'whichever way you throw me I shall stand'. The Isle of Man is an independent island, you see. We always have been and we still stand firm whoever comes, whatever happens, whatever we have to do. We have our own government, our own laws and our own way of doing things.'

'Thank you.' Mother crossed to my side then and hurried me out of the shop. She stood on the pavement, silent, staring ahead. 'That woman's just told me about someone I should go and see,' she murmured. 'She lives in a house called 'Wave Crest' near the Queen's Pier on the South Promenade. Come on. Let's see if we can find it.'

Having no idea where we were going or why, I followed Mother until we stood on the sea front.

'This must be it,' she said, pointing to a small, whitewashed cottage facing the sea. The house, which stood alone behind a low wall, boasted pale blue woodwork. It had four little windows but no front door. Instead a stony path led to the right side of the house where, beneath a porch, we could just see a narrow door.

'Well, we're here now,' said Mother straightening her shoulders, 'so we may as well … come on.' Nervously I followed her up the path. Mother knocked on the door.

'Come in,' a voice called. 'It's open.' Slowly Mother pushed at the door and I followed, by now even more apprehensive. 'And shut the door,' the voice continued.

We stepped straight into a small dark room. The tiny windowpanes let in very little light. A narrow staircase circled upwards from the far corner and at its base some chairs stood round a circular wooden table, against which leaned the woman who'd bade us enter. She was thin and, to my eyes, old and witch-like, with long, straggly grey hair framing her face. Her clothes appeared grey and shapeless too. She stared at us and then, without warning, she burst into tears, collapsing into a chair and rocking backwards and forwards as she cried and moaned. I was terrified. My knees buckled and I backed away, feeling for the door behind me. I grabbed at the cold metal latch, desperate to escape.

'Oh, I'm in such trouble,' the woman cried, 'such trouble!' That was too much for Mother. She stepped forward.

'*You're* in trouble,' she began indignantly, but the woman stretched out her hand.

'I know, my dear, I know. Sit down.' Then as Mother sank into a chair, she went on, 'I know all about it. My tears are your tears, my dear.' There was a pause as she sat up and dried her eyes, then continued, 'But he's here, you know. He's still with you in his Air Force uniform. Your man's standing beside you, by your right shoulder. I see him so clearly.' I stared at Mother sitting straight-backed and alone in her chair.

'He smiles and I see where he lost a front tooth. He's still with you, you see, and he always will be, my dear. He wants you to know that.'

In my terror, I heard no more. I was desperate to leave, but I couldn't. I was still pressed back against the wooden door, the old-fashioned latch behind me cutting into my fingers. I had to wait while the conversation continued, now just a murmur, but I believe that Mother found it comforting. Then they both stood up. I snatched the door open and I heard the woman say firmly, 'Go to Athol Street. Go to Athol Street in Douglas. They'll help you.'

The interview over, we found ourselves outside Wave Crest. I ran down the path and across the promenade, still shivering. Mother followed more slowly and there was silence as she gazed down at the sea gently lapping against the wall she leaned on. I waited for her to speak. To my right I could see a long iron pier, which seemed to stretch miles out to sea.

'Athol Street, now where's that?' Mother said quietly at last.

'Athol Street? Oh, that's up that way, off the top of Prospect Hill,' said a man in Douglas when we stopped to ask directions. Prospect Hill: in hindsight, a fitting name. There on the left, two or three doors along, we stumbled into the offices of the Royal Air Force Benevolent Fund. It was strange if nobody at Jurby had told Mother about it. But now we were there, facing a kindly man across a desk. The help and advice he gave, none of which I understood, helped Mother to find her feet and set our lives in some sort of order. In fact the organisation was to help again years later, when I was given a grant so that I might travel 'across' to take up a course at College. We shall always be grateful to them, but more gratitude must go to our strange counsellor.

'We really ought to go back to Wave Crest,' said Mother a few weeks later. 'She was so helpful.'

'I'm not going in!' Wild horses wouldn't get me inside that cottage again.

'No, you can stay outside, but I must go and thank her.'

But this time nobody answered the door, nobody bade us enter. As we made our way back down the path, a woman passing with a pram said, 'Oh, you won't find anyone there. She was taken to a nursing home about a week ago – Douglas, I think.'

So we never again saw 'Moll Doone', as Mother christened her. Mother never succeeded in tracking her down and Wave Crest has long since gone. But what remained is the belief that we are never truly alone. I know that gave Mother strength and I know she always believed in my father's presence. When I grew up, I was for years sceptical, but several similar inexplicable events later in my life were to convince me that perhaps she was right after all. It had only needed 'Moll Doone' to point it out to us in the first place.

* * *

Before we could finally begin to put down new roots, Mother had to return to Cheshire once more. It was late August, barely two months since the world turned upside down and so, of course, I went with her, although I didn't know the exact reasons for the visit.

'While we're there we'll go and see Grandma and Grandad,' said Mother. That seemed such a good idea and all the way on the bus to Manchester I looked forward to seeing my paternal grandparents again. Both Mother's parents died when she was a child. In this strange new adult world of packing and form filling and quiet conversations, it would be lovely to feel Grandma's warm hug.

'Do you think they'll let me play 'Twinkle, Twinkle' on the piano like Daddy and me ...?' I began excitedly. Then realising what I'd said I ended lamely, 'or p'raps Grandad will let me see his big silver watch, then I can show him I can still tell the time.'

'Perhaps,' Mother answered absently, 'but you mustn't bother them too much.'

As the bus took us nearer to the tall terraced houses of Moss Side, I stared out of the window and thought about Grandma's cosy kitchen. The high walls of the back yard, where Grandad kept his window cleaning ladders, made it hard for the sun to peep through the windows, but it was always a warm and friendly room. A kettle steamed quietly beside the big black-leaded range and high above it on the mantelpiece all sorts of interesting things jostled for space. A black clock ticked gently in the centre, while tins sat at each end. The one on the left was fat and square, while that on the right was tall and thin. The tall tin was full of buttons, which I loved to play with, sorting them into their different shapes and colours. Perhaps Grandma would let me do that today. Filling in the spaces between tins and clock there was a little cat made of plaster nestling against a ball of string with scissors poking up from the centre; a hair brush and comb; an odd looking model of a bird with a broken beak and Grandad's glasses which he could never find; and behind it all were letters and bills, bits of paper and envelopes, most wilting and discoloured as they waited for attention which they would probably never get.

'Here we are.' Mother's voice broke into my thoughts. I ran up the short path and banged on the door, eager to see Grandma again.

Grandad opened the door and without a word enveloped us both in a silent hug. Then, his mouth quivering, he nodded towards the kitchen and ushered us in.

'Here's Pops and Ann to see us,' he said to my grandmother. I ran into the room then stopped. The cosy kitchen I expected was now cold and dim, for the fire was low and the curtains were half drawn against the light.

'She won't have them open,' Grandad murmured, 'not since ...' He moved across and gently put a hand on his wife's shoulder. Grandma sat beside the fireplace, grey, quiet and crumpled, her slippered feet against ashes, which had fallen from the grate. She didn't turn or speak to us, just rocked back and forth as she stared ahead, seeing nothing. 'I'll make us some tea,' he continued. 'She doesn't do much at the moment. Come on, Ann, you can help me.' The room seemed so sad that I was glad to go into the back kitchen with him, though neither of us could think of anything to say. I just 'helped' Grandad by finding teaspoons and setting out a few biscuits. I could hear low voices in the other room, but never knew what was said. I only knew that everyone, except poor sad Grandad, was glad when our brief visit ended.

The next day we arrived in a stormy Fleetwood to find that bad weather had cancelled the afternoon sailing. We were marooned on the dockside, a small woman not much bigger than the child who clutched her hand, a pile of luggage and very little money. Grimly, Mother marched us along some streets and into a police station. She plonked our luggage down on the floor.

'We can't get a boat till tomorrow,' she said to the policeman frowning down at us from behind his counter, 'so you'll have to find us somewhere to stay. I don't know the place, but if you can't get us in somewhere, we'll have to stay here.' I gazed round the bare, high-ceilinged room flanked by uncomfortable looking brown benches round the walls. 'And it'll have to be cheap.' Faced by such fierce determination, someone found us a bed to share in a cold boarding house several streets away.

By 8 o'clock the next morning, we were back at the quayside. Rain and gale force winds swept mercilessly across the bleak landing stage now peopled by other miserable travellers, nearly all clad in khaki or air-force blue. It was to be a nightmare journey, for the sea was in defiant mood.

'Down below, down below!' Sailors, already hanging on to their caps, pushed us all down the steep, narrow, ladder-like steps, away from the greasy deck and into the holds below.

'Come on love. I'll pop you both up here,' said a burly soldier, and he lifted Mother and me up on to the top of a high pile of kitbags against the metal wall.

For the next six hours (two hours longer than scheduled) we clung to our perch, while below us men in khaki lay on the heaving deck and wished to die.

I was too frightened to feel sick. I just shut my eyes, clung to the kitbags and longed to be on dry land again, but this was a journey we had to take. There was no alternative.

The boat plunged away from Fleetwood to do battle with the Irish Sea. Angry waves forced themselves through cracks round the heavy, rusty looking iron doors. If the ship ever had stabilisers, they were useless now. Everyone was ill. Only the Manx sailors seemed immune as they staggered from deck to deck, struggling to step over prone figures to collect tickets while chivvying their passengers with indecent cheerfulness.

'Tickets please! Come on now, where's your ticket?' Greeted by moans, they were generally forced to bend down and find it for themselves. It was not a journey to endear anyone to the sea. Even the road seemed to rock as we staggered to the little train we were getting to know so well, and we finally arrived 'home' just glad to be alive. At that moment, we didn't care what the island was like or even what future lay ahead. The ground didn't move beneath our feet and that was enough.

Chapter 6

*D*ropping my load of sticks by the back door, I bounded into the kitchen. I'd spent the afternoon combing the fields opposite the house for firewood. Coal was expensive as well as in short supply. It was satisfying to find old branches tossed to the ground by the wind and I soon learned how ripe they were and if they were ready to burn, by the snap they made when broken beneath my foot. Solid ones were dragged home through long grass, to await breaking or sawing later. I rarely, if ever, saw anyone in those small fields bordered by untidy, straggled hedges. It was a safe and splendid education in all aspects of country lore. This time I'd been out on my own, for Mother had a pile of ironing to face and Ruff had already expended his energy earlier in the day.

'Off you go, but don't be long,' Mother had said, her face flushed as she bent to retrieve the small flat iron from the fire. She spat on its base. There was a satisfying hiss and the spit rolled off and dropped into space. 'I'll stay and finish this and then it's done with.' She sat the iron in its thin metal slipper, snapped the clip shut across it and dragged my green skirt on to the ironing board. 'Just be careful, and don't be too long or you'll miss 'Children's Hour', she added.

The BBC, with its medium and long wave stations was our link with the outside world, as long as we remembered to keep the battery-driven wireless in working order. This meant taking the accumulator (wet battery) to Ramsey each week for recharging, while we borrowed another to keep us going in the meantime.

Tuning in regularly to favourite programmes formed a pattern to the days. With breakfast we had Kitchen Front food hints, and Gert and Daisy's recipes, sometimes advice from the Radio Doctor, and then to help with the housework, Music While You Work, a half hour programme broadcast every morning and afternoon. Workers' Playtime entertained us at lunchtime and there were a variety of comedy shows in the evenings, as well as the must-listen-to News broadcasts. I listened regularly to Children's Hour and enjoyed Larry the Lamb and Mr Growser in 'Toytown'.

On Tuesdays we had tea at 5 o'clock so that I could learn more about the countryside by going 'Out with Romany' along with Doris and Jack the spaniel. Now, on returning, I found the kitchen empty, but I could hear voices in the front room. I pushed open the door.

Mother sat sideways on the edge of an armchair and a man sat hunched in the chair opposite. He was wearing a cream raincoat and on his knee he clutched a long black book. He turned.

'Ah, so this is your daughter,' he said.

'Yes.' Mother looked a bit flustered as she turned to me. 'This is the School Attendance Officer. He thinks you should be at school.'

'Come, come,' the man said gently. 'You know I'm right. Under the circumstances I can understand you wanting her here with you, but it just won't do now, will it?' He looked at us and shook his head. Mother stood up.

'No, of course not,' she replied. 'She will be in school next week. Thank you for calling.'

There was no point in arguing. We both knew that I'd escaped for long enough. This was just another step in returning to 'normal', and since I knew what school was like now, I wasn't too worried about going there. It had been very different when I first started three years earlier.

Daddy had seemed to think it was a good idea. 'There'll be lots of books to read,' he'd said enthusiastically, and he should know. Working for a newspaper before the war, he loved words in any form. 'And games to play and new children to play with.'

But that was the problem. The books and games were all right, but I hadn't wanted to meet new children. I hated that and got an 'excited pain' in the tummy even at the thought of it, especially if it was to be at a party. But I had to give school a try, so nervously I'd held my teacher's hand and ventured into the great unknown. That day had seemed awfully long and I only felt safe with Miss Probert – which meant that whenever she left the room, I had to go too. It was years before Mother told me that during those first few weeks the teachers referred to me as Miss Probert's little lamb. At teatime, Daddy had leaned across the table and said, 'Well, how was school? Did you like it?'

'No,' I said. 'I'm not going there again. We didn't learn anything,' and I never knew why he laughed. So,

Top: Sulby School, the Girls' entrance on the right.
Above, right: Infants' classroom, 1990s, with Senior room beyond.
Above, left: St Stephen's Church and Church Hall.

in late September 1942, four days before my eighth birthday, Mother and I set off on a chilly morning to join different pupils, this time in Sulby School.

This was on the Straight, about a fifteen-minute walk away from home. First opened in 1879, the lofty, high-windowed Victorian building had two large classrooms divided by a glass partition, which rattled when you leaned on it. Facing them, and sandwiched between cloakrooms on either side, there was a smaller room. Being an unknown quantity, I went into the 'little ones' room for assessment. The day had started and we arrived late. Mother pushed me gently into the room where everyone sat primly in his place and all eyes turned on the new girl carrying a small square cardboard box and, as directed, her plimsolls to change into on wet days. Miss Craine, the Infants' teacher rose from her desk and, smiling, beckoned me over.

'This is Ann,' she said kindly, nodding to Mother over my head, so that she backed away and left. 'Now, let's find you a seat,' and she indicated a low chair behind an equally low table against the partition. She took my coat and the gas mask case, and added softly, 'you needn't bring your gas mask to school, dear. You won't need it here.' Then she perched on a nearby chair and asked, 'Did you have to use it often?'

'Yes, we had to practise in school.' Even looking at the box made me feel breathless.

'Shall we show it to the little ones and tell them about it?'

'I don't have to put it on, do I?' I felt panic rising at the thought. I knew that the mask's cloying rubbery smell would make me gasp and take my breath away. I always felt it would stop me breathing.

'No, of course not if you don't want to.' Miss Craine lifted the thing out of the box and began to explain why people thought it might be needed and how it worked. 'You put your chin in here and the strap goes behind your head.'

Slowly I began to tell them about going down into the air-raid shelter when the siren went. And it reminded me of how shocked I'd been when a few months earlier I'd walked into the pantry under the stairs in our old home. It had been converted into our own air-raid shelter complete with a camp-bed, blankets, tins of food, a pickaxe, other tools and a bucket of sand.

'From school we went across the road and down some steps. The shelter was made of cold concrete, and there were no windows and only one light bulb. We had to sit on benches against the walls.'

'Did you do your lessons there?' someone asked.

'Not really. We used to sing the letters of the alphabet, and sometimes that made the mask's window steam up, but if you rubbed soap on the inside it wasn't so bad. And if you breathed in suddenly you made a rude noise.'

One of the boys wanted to try that and he eventually succeeded in making a farting sound. Everyone laughed.

'That's enough now.' Miss Craine put the gas mask away and I breathed freely again. At dinnertime I thrust the box at Mother.

'I don't have to take this any more.' So it was put to the back of the wardrobe and I don't remember ever seeing it again.

Miss Craine was tall and spare, with a wide smile and a gentle, loving manner. She was a good teacher, firm and fair, and the Infants' good behaviour and learning were taught through kind but effective methods. Jean, with her pretty little turned up nose and tight brown curls, squabbled with Ethel over an Arithmetic card. It had a picture of a pram on the top and they both wanted it.

'It's mine!'

'No, I had it first! Give it here!'

They pulled and the card tore down the middle, leaving them horrified and embarrassed. For punishment, they each had to stand on their low chairs side by side in the corner of the room, holding the card together so that it formed a whole again.

'See what naughty girls we have today,' Miss Craine admonished quietly.

The teacher's desk was the focal point of the room. It was set at an angle beside an open fire, which in winter roared behind a high fireguard. On a cold, wet morning it was a positive joy to line up to have work marked: to stand, legs burning from the heat, beside mittens and socks which quietly steamed along the top of the fireguard. The room was furnished with tiny tables and chairs. Pictures, illustrated number charts and alphabets gleamed on the walls, and puzzles and games tumbled from shelves beneath a library of books. There was a big blackboard and easel and at Christmas, a fine decorated tree. This was 'home' to everyone in Sulby and the surrounding area for the first three years of his educational life.

All too soon, I was 'sent up' to the top class on the other side of the partition. Here, aged eight or nine, one graduated from desks near the partition, across the room to end up at the far wall near the piano at the ripe old age of eleven.

Here in 'the big ones' classroom, life was colder and less cheery. The grate remained unused and one large, mobile paraffin stove tried its best to warm the room, but its heat drifted up into high rafters above, leaving us on a cold winter's day gloved and coated below. It was dustier than the Infants' room, having two high blackboards standing on easels, one at either side of the room. There were bulging cupboards beneath piles of books, and on the walls large World maps, shiny and palely coloured. Everyone knew that the cane resting across the mantelpiece at the front of the class could be used to effect. Punishment was meted out, not by gentle words, but by lines, detentions or, for the boys, several strokes of that cane across the palm of the hand. The desks were double desks with bench seats, which meant that if you forgot to step into the aisle when you stood up, your neighbour was forced to stand too with buckled knees. A large sepia portrait of the Victorian Manx poet, T.E.Brown, gazed down on us from the back wall. Having published several books of poetry, he was revered. His claim to fame included verses beginning:

'A garden is a lovesome thing, God wot ...'

A sentiment echoed by the Headmaster on bad days.

Mr Allen, the Headmaster and also the 'big ones' teacher, was a pale-faced, rotund, irascible man. Unofficially known as 'Pop', he peered short-sightedly at the world through small round glasses. He could be a strict disciplinarian, depending on his mood, but when the bigger boys got too much for him, he would roar, 'Right! Get out the spades. You'll do the next hour on the allotment!' – an order welcomed by most of the miscreants. Sometimes he demanded instead that the Schoolhouse garden be weeded, but whatever it was, it was a diversion from lessons – though not generally for the girls. The allotment was across the road from the school. Apart from answering the Government's call to 'Dig for Victory', its purpose was twofold: to teach us the rudiments of gardening, which most of the others in school knew anyway, and to provide fresh food for sale, an example of a self-financing business.

Even though it was not very big, here grew all the usual vegetables – potatoes, cabbage, carrots, onions, beans and peas, peas so sweet and satisfying when opened with a resounding 'pop' to see if they were 'ready'. A few fruit bushes completed the picture, though strangely, it was only the gooseberries which in the end had enough fruit left for selling. We were the customers, after offerings had been made to the Harvest Festival in St Stephen's Church next door. We bore home our purchases proudly, our token payments going toward seeds for next year, though I'm sure that the Schoolhouse kitchen received a large share of the produce as 'teacher's perks'. But for us the allotment's real value lay in its escape route from lessons, especially when 'Pop' was so irritated that he sent the girls out too, instead of leaving us indoors, with Miss Craine to help in our battle with sewing needles. On other occasions when he felt he needed a break, 'Pop' would growl 'Carry on. No talking, I'll be back in a minute,' open the door between the classrooms, nod to his teacher and then disappear into the schoolhouse for a cup of tea. I soon discovered, however, that in wartime, the autumn season gave us all official time off.

'Unless it's wet, the school will be closed on Wednesday afternoon.'

The announcement was greeted by excited shuffling, barely subdued whoops of joy and silent prayers for fine weather. 'Bring your rose-hips in on Thursday morning.' So the hedgerows were plundered for fat red hips to be made into syrup rich in vitamin C. We never wondered where our bounty actually went for processing and bottling. We were just glad that the task coincided with the blackberry season. Once we had gathered enough hips to merit our time off, we turned to fruit picking, returning home with hands and mouth stained a fine shade of purple. The government would have been pleased to know how diligently we gathered the Hedgerow Harvest.

In fact, although EllanVannin is a self-governing island, it followed England and did its best to ensure that its children remained healthy in spite of war. We were all regularly weighed and measured by the school doctor in the small room which opened off the top classroom. We were subjected to various ear and eye tests and occasional dental inspections, and any child found to have the skin complaint impetigo had Gentian Violet painted over the spots, the colour staying with him for days. At morning playtime we were expected to drink our daily third of a pint of milk. In winter, if the crate hadn't first been placed by Miss Craine's fire, the milk sometimes sat an inch above the bottle in a little frozen column beneath its cardboard top. We were also exhorted to 'remind mother to get your cod liver oil and malt', something I enjoyed. A sticky spoonful, tasting like melted toffee, was a treat on a wintry morning when you'd used up all your sweet rations. The malt was certainly preferable to Scott's Emulsion, which Mother tried to administer. The sou-westered fisherman on the label, grinning as he shouldered a huge fish, was warning enough and the white glutinous mixture made my stomach heave. Nor did I fare much better with Syrup of Figs guaranteed to 'keep you regular'.

About once a term a whisper would hurry round the classroom – 'I've just heard her car!' and everyone wriggled expectantly, for this meant another diversion in the form of the 'nit nurse'. We shuffled into line for fingernail and hair inspections from the travelling school nurse and the unfortunate child told to step out of line had the embarrassment of knowing that head lice had been spotted. Only once did this happen to me. Mother was aghast and I had to endure shampoos, which involved liberal applications of paraffin, to clear them. From then on, my long curls, hitherto carefully rolled into 'curlie rags' every night, were combed briskly with a very fine comb before being pulled back sharply into plaits, and I was frequently reminded not to put my head near anyone else's.

All in all, Sulby School was a happy place, the pupils generally easy going and tolerant, and I soon made friends, especially with Ethel and Jean, the tearers of work cards. Ethel lived next door, was slightly older than I was and proved to be a useful friend, for she had older brothers who could be relied upon to tower threateningly over anyone who troubled their sister. I think curiosity was the main reason behind the first time she knocked on the door to escort me to school. After all, there weren't many 'come-overs' in Sulby. We played together, she showed me where the best wild cherries grew. Then, having counted them out into two ruby-rich piles on our concrete path warmed by the summer sun, we munched our way through them and planned some other game. We exchanged toys and comics on short-term loan, generally amicably.

'Can I have my Beano back?' I asked once.

'I haven't got it'. But I knew better because I could see it under her coat. I grabbed it, slapped her face and rushed into the house to cry, whether from anger or embarrassment, I can't remember.

Jean, on the other hand, one of seven children, lived in a small semi detached cottage about a mile away, near Sulby Bridge at the far end of the village. But to us, distance was never a barrier. From the beginning I liked her ready smile, which crinkled up her nose and I envied her her sisters. She in turn, wished for my single child status and clothes or toys which had never been handed down. So in a pact of mutual envy and admiration, we began a friendship, which was to last for the rest of our lives. We trotted up and down the distance that separated us, generally pushing doll's prams, playing, exploring or paddling in the river. At teatime, we'd walk each other home up the Straight – 'I'll come half way with you.' Then, when the halfway stage was reached, 'I'll come half way back with you.' We must have looked a funny pair tracing and retracing our steps.

A few weeks after I'd started school, I arrived home for tea to find Mother sitting beside the kitchen fire. Her feet rested on the brass fender, which I remembered from our old home, and the little square, leather-topped metal buffets which always sat at either end were there too, open and empty.

'There's a nice surprise for you in there,' she said and pointed to a long narrow cupboard, which lay to the right of the fireplace. I snatched open the door and to my delight, Teddy and Golly, my two favourite soft toys fell out, along with one or two games and a couple of books. Then Mother added, 'Your doll's pram and my machine have come, too, so I can finish off your coat now.' She smiled as I hugged her. I looked forward to having my new coat. In a rich blue fabric, it was begun before we moved, and I'd chosen blue buttons, which looked like tiny tyroleon hats painted with a little red feather. Then Mother added sadly, 'But Mrs Booth put the china in the buffets, and I'm afraid it's all broken.'

So the remains of her precious tea service and

treasured ornaments were wrapped in paper and buried, and for years we continued to use the odd bits of crockery already in the bungalow. Burying the china was not some form of morbid funeral. Without realising it, we were ahead of our time and 'environmentally friendly', for in the countryside there was neither dustbin nor collection. Consequently, to avoid encouraging the 'big fellas' (rats), anything that would burn went on the fire. We had no compost heap, although since we had no time to cultivate the garden it wouldn't have been used anyway. Vegetable peelings, wrapped tightly in paper, laid at the back of the fire and covered by the gritty dust of coal slack, will maintain heat for quite a while – and save coal. Food waste was burned too, on the rare occasion when it was not collected by a local farmer for his pigs or boiled up for the hens' mash. Even empty food tins were burned before being flattened and buried in the garden.

In fact, in our house there was no waste whatsoever. Economy was the watchword and everything was recycled. Since clothing needed coupons (66 allocated each year, a dress on average took 11 and a coat 16) Mother's sewing machine was in constant use. Not only was she able to make clothes for us both, but existing garments were 'modified' and collars and cuffs turned to hide any fraying. As I grew in every direction in the clean country air dresses were 'let out' and skirts lengthened. Other more utilitarian items came in for the same treatment. When holes appeared in our pre-war linens and towels they were repaired. If a sheet, it was sliced down the middle, turned and joined one side to the other. When that gave way, any whole fabric left was made into pillowcases. A towel's life cycle extended from new to threadbare, to dish cloth, floor cloth, duster, or cat's bedding, before being consigned to the flames. Jars and 'nice' tins were never thrown away, because they might be useful as containers. My small contribution to the housekeeping was to gather wood and sift the cinders. In an occasional bout of extravagance when clearing out the grate, we sometimes threw out decent sized cinders with the ashes. So I regularly disappeared down the garden with a small round sieve to rake through the ash patch and triumphantly sieve out the bigger cinders, which were used again on the fire.

We followed the government's example when it came to re-using paper. Wartime envelopes were recycled. A square of paper bearing the order 'War Economy, Re-use' was stuck over the original address and then folded over the previously opened edge, where, at the back, we were informed that 'Patriotism (in capital letters) as well as economy demand the use of these envelope savers. A general use of them would save thousands of tons of shipping.' There was sometimes a V for victory in each bottom corner. In fact, we were careful to save and recycle all paper. If not used on the fire or in the toilet, it was smoothed – sometimes even ironed – and re-used; string was carefully un-knotted from its parcel and wound into a little ball for next time; woollen garments were painstakingly unpicked, the wool wound into hanks round my outstretched hands before being washed, stretched, hung out to dry and then knitted up again. Socks were darned until there was more darn than sock and shoes had Philips' stick-on soles. We threw little away and I still can't, much to the frustration of my family.

Chapter 7

*U*ntil the war was over, there was never any question of having visits from anyone, not even the family. But we still had occasional visitors from the aerodrome mainly Sid, a 'regular' at the camp who'd become a friend of my father's. It was he who had apologetically brought back the bicycle and he turned up now and again to see if we needed help with anything. So he put up a new washing line and tried to persuade the front gate not to drag its feet and then rolled up his sleeves to turn the 'garage' into a more useful building. That was the corrugated iron shed at the bottom of the garden, yards from the gate and never used for vehicles.

'Next spring,' Mother announced, 'we're going to keep hens in here. I'll ask about getting straw and we must look for some strong branches to make perches. We may as well have our own fresh eggs if we can.'

A few days later, and a wet playtime, I was in the girls' cloakroom scrubbing my hands. Although classes were mixed, Sulby School saw segregation in cloakrooms, the playground and in some lessons in the final years. The cloakroom for the girls and Infants, with its coat pegs and two low wash-basins, lay behind the first classroom and beyond this, was the girls' playground with toilets at the end. This rough area of tarmac and gravel, a splinter of which still rests in my hand, was divided, like a continuation of the indoor partition, by a high wall separating the sexes. The boys' playground and toilets were on their side of the great divide. Consequently there was much jumping up to scrape knees and shoes on the centre wall, but trouble threatened anyone foolish enough to cross the boundary, and nobody ever did. It was more fun to hurl abuse and catcalls as we tried to guess what was happening on the other side.

So, because I was Ink Monitor for the top class that day, I began playtime trying to scrub my fingers clean of ink beneath the girls' cold-water tap. Being monitor involved stirring the liquid (which settled in a sediment at the bottom of its brown pottery jug) before pouring it messily into small china inkwells. These sat beneath brass caps in allotted holes at each end of every desk. Even the liberal use of blotting paper failed to keep the wretched stuff under control and every child had stained fingers for days, even though it was reputed to be washable ink.

As I scrubbed, rain began to beat on the windows and in no time the small cloakroom was full of damp girls, most of them older than I was. As steam misted the window, I became aware that for some reason, I was the centre of attention. Then suddenly,

'I thought your Dad was dead,' said Alma, leaning nonchalantly against the wall behind me. 'Who was that man in your garden on Sunday?'

Startled and rather embarrassed at being questioned so directly, I said, 'Oh, Mother's friend.'

'Who?' asked Betty, one of the oldest girls in the school. I repeated my reply.

'Oh, I see — Mother's *friend*,' said Alma pointedly and sniggers rippled round the coat pegs. 'He's Mother's friend, girls!'

I felt my face go scarlet though I didn't know why. Then Dorothy, Jean's elder sister, came to my rescue.

'Shut up, you two,' she said, 'and mind your own business.' She turned to me. 'Take no notice of that lot. They're just being nosey.'

I didn't report the incident to Mother, but it was soon evident that she knew there was speculation about the few callers we had, especially since they generally wore RAF uniform. Under the circumstances that was hardly surprising. We were strangers and in a village on an island everyone was interested in everyone else's business, especially in the 1940s. But my mother was a proud woman and if there was one thing she couldn't stand, it was unfounded gossip which besmirched a reputation. So, with me trotting behind as usual, she strode into the village shop, all

4ft 7ins of her, the doorbell jangling imperiously as we arrived. Two customers swung round and Maggie, the shop-keeper, stopped mid-sentence with her mouth open.

'I understand there's gossip in the village about me and my family,' Mother began and you could almost see sparks outlining her indignant little body. 'I am here to say that if I hear any more of it, I shall sue for defamation of character. You'd better pass that on in your gossip.'

Leaving shock and a sheepish silence in our wake, we left as abruptly as we'd entered. Thereafter, Mother was known as 'a little tiger' best left out of gossip, and for some time I was viewed with pity for having a harridan for a mother. But it was only because of such strength that she was able to survive. In subsequent years, as she began to join in village life, this was forgotten and when she finally moved away from Sulby she was a liked and respected member of the community.

So the months passed and I at least, slowly integrated into village life and got to know some of our neighbours. The postman, Bobby, lived at the crossroads and rode a bicycle, or leaned on it as he pushed it along when his legs tired of pedalling. We looked for him every day, hoping for letters from the aunts or family friends 'across'. We never had to read a postcard for he'd comment on it as he passed it over.

' Looks a nice place, that. Pity it's raining.' But more often than not he would shake his head mournfully when he saw us and drawl, 'Nothin' today at all. No, no, nothin' today,' and slowly move on.

The pebble-dashed post office, with the shop and the station, were the centres for all news. And it was a very efficient service, for Fred, the stationmaster and Maggie, the shop-keeper were man and wife, while little Florrie in the post office kept the news circulating with her fellow gossips. Heads would nod and old lady whiskers shake as it was examined and clucked over, and phrases like 'Yes, Yes,' Never!' 'Well, I always said…' would crowd the air. After Mother's announcement, Maggie took care that we were never party to any gossip, and we were served quickly and courteously, which in a way was a pity. Still, if there was anything interesting going on, we generally heard of it eventually through the invisible village grapevine. We soon came to realise, too, that it was not wise to discuss anyone with a third party, for most people were inter-related, though they might not disclose that at the time.

One of the more friendly places in the village was our railway station and travelling to and from there became a pleasure.

Part of the enchantment for me came from the sharp contrast between this small, friendly country station and the noisy, impersonal and overcrowded ones I could remember in England: stations which seemed dark and overshadowed by an aura of departures and unhappiness.

Fred was in sole charge here and he was usually to be found idling along the short platform of the single-track line with his hands in his pockets and a pipe in his mouth. He was a short, sandy-haired man, always

Sulby Glen Station, here converted to a dwelling after the demise of the northern route, its picket fence crossing the track and Fred's office window beside the foliage.

affable and unflustered, nodding in agreement to whatever was said. 'Ay. Ay' was his reply to most remarks. In the high-ceilinged waiting room, where ivy had grown up to peep in through dusty windows, only visitors tapped vainly on the ticket office window and expected it to open. It never did, for everyone automatically turned left across the echoing wooden floor to enter Fred's office, an untidy, cosy little den. Here a cheerful fire glowed permanently in the small triangular fireplace opposite the door – doubtless one of the perks of being part of a steam-driven railway. To the right of the fire, under a window facing the road, stood a high slanting wooden desk littered with Fred's pipes, papers, and the stationmaster's red and green flags. A tall stool at the desk waited for Fred to perch upon it as he watched the world go by, in between welcoming and waving off his travellers and the self-important little trains.

'Oh, there goes young Bobby, it must be dinnertime,' he'd say as a stocky young man walked past with bowed head and rolling gait – 'young' Bobby as opposed to the postman. 'He used to be on the boats, you know.' This Bobby was a painfully shy bachelor and when we said 'Hallo', just to see if he'd answer, he'd go red with embarrassment. If he did speak, the sound of his voice seemed to startle him and he'd quickly walk on. So, under Fred's guidance, we gradually got to know the villagers, and being a child, it was easy for me to become accepted by them. One of the first to speak to me was Mr Caine, an old man who lived in a big house nearly opposite ours.

'Hallo,' he said over the gate as I hurried home from somewhere. 'Do you like tomatoes?' Then, since I must have looked doubtful, he added, 'Go and ask your mother if you can come and get some.' Together, Mother and I went across the road and into a big greenhouse, which stood against the wall at the side of his house. It was the first time I'd ever entered one. I was surprised by its damp and warmth and especially by the overpowering, and new to me, smell of fresh tomatoes, tumbling in profusion down the stems of their plants. It was a smell always to be associated with that greenhouse.

Later, when he came to know us better, he suggested that like him, we kept a goat. 'It won't cost much, ' he said. 'You've got a big garden and it'll eat the grass and any old scraps, and if you get a Nanny, you can milk her.' Mother drew the line at that, but did decide to try the idea. She acquired two Billy goats, but they didn't understand their place in the family and didn't stay long. They disliked being tethered. They roamed, they smelled, they followed us around and butted us with horns and rock-like heads. Mr Caine was right – they did eat anything, even our clothes if we got too near to them. Ruff was not the only one glad to see them go.

We did, however, have some success with about half a dozen hens housed in the garage. Over the years we had various breeds – White Leghorns, Rhode Island Reds, creamy Light Sussex and a strange black breed with a little plume of feathers nodding on the top of their heads. We began with a few mature hens then decided to expand.

'Next spring we'll get some chicks,' said Mother enthusiastically, 'we haven't enough eggs to hatch our own.'

Our first dozen chicks arrived by train in a neat square box with a perforated lid, beneath which lay a hoop of white cardboard to prevent the creatures becoming trapped in the corners. We immediately fell in love with these tiny, cheeping balls of yellow fluff. They looked so fragile, and the broody hen chosen to be mother in a specially made cage didn't seem too sure about them. But as we introduced them one by one, she began to cluck happily and pushed them under her feathers with a gentle beak.

'I think we'll get a rooster next,' Mother said with

satisfaction. 'Then we can breed our own chicks.'

So various bumptious cockerels joined the family from time to time. They preened their magnificent, shiny coloured feathers, strutted with importance as they kept their harem in order, and woke us at dawn with their crowing.

Occasionally a hen would lay away from the official straw lined boxes in the shed. Feeling broodiness coming on, she'd try to outwit us by disappearing into the nearby field to keep her clutch of eggs to herself. She was safe enough, unless attacked by a stray dog, for there were no foxes on the Isle of Man – or squirrels or moles come to that – but she just wasn't playing the game. So she was either rewarded with an official nursery for her hatching, or a cage with a slatted floor, its discomfort soon chasing away her broodiness. One, deciding to limit her family, deserted the last two eggs in the nest. We brought them in and set them on a soft cloth in the top oven by the fire. After a few hours one egg began to rock gently and then to crack.

'Can I hold it?' I asked breathlessly. Then, as I did so the chick continued to peck its way out of the shell, until at last it flopped, straggly, wet and exhausted into the palm of my hand. I felt it was an honour to have watched such a miracle.

As well as keeping us in eggs for much of the year – and each autumn we preserved some of the bounty in a bucket of isinglass – the birds provided us with the luxury of a chicken dinner. I well remember Mother, red-faced, hair on end, scurrying round the garden, arms outstretched after a bird literally fleeing for its life.

'Quick! Quick!' she screamed. 'Catch that broiler!' Eventually it was cornered. Then Mother took hen and courage in both hands. Tucking the bird under one arm, she walked round the garden, looking skyward until she had succeeded in wringing its neck. Then, just to make sure, she'd always sever head from body with a swift blow of the axe and we'd pray that it wouldn't flap round as the nerves died – it often did. So comes the saying about flapping around like a headless chicken.

Mother particularly disliked this aspect of our new life, so different from that she'd been used to. But as she said when she struggled to skin her first rabbit (given to us by George and Julia), 'What else can I do? I've no choice. We have to eat.'

I only once tried to skin a rabbit. It's a very slippery business and not advised for the squeamish. I think it's those great innocent eyes, which seem to watch you even when lifeless. There's a knack to the task, and if you're well practised it's possible to remove the fur as a complete pelt. I wasn't and couldn't. My rabbit was all over the kitchen table, slipping and sliding until we both ended up on the floor. At which point I gave up and agreed only to pluck chickens.

We had met George and Julia, who went 'pea-ing' in their own fields (pea-picking), several times and learned that Irish Julia had been happily married to Manxman George for many years. They lived about a quarter of a mile away from us on the road to Jurby, in a tiny, two up, two down stone built cottage. Another adjoining them had been empty for years. They sat behind a hedge of old fashioned, full-blown pink roses, but even their perfume couldn't mask farmyard smells rising from a weedy garden to the side of Julia's house. There several hens scratched and a pig rootled around in deep mud. Late one afternoon George invited us in for a cup of tea. The front door was practically on the road, so it took only a couple of steps to meet a flight of stairs just inside the front door and another step to the right to enter their now darkening kitchen/living room.

'The dim's coming on middlin' early tonight,' observed George, with a typical old Manx turn of phrase.

'He means the dusk,' said Julia.

Facing us was a large old-fashioned range where a fire burned brightly. A table sat beneath a low window to the right and to the left a sofa pressed against the wall behind the big pram we'd seen before. Here we saw their daughter, to whom they had devoted their lives. Now grown and in her teens, she lay spread-eagled in the pram, or rather half out of it. Following our gaze, Julia turned to look her with a wry smile. 'That's Ruth,' she said. 'She was a normal baby till she was nearly a year. Then one day someone,' her lips tightened, '…when someone was bathing her, she slipped and fell on her head on the floor.'

'Concrete,' murmured George.

'Well, it damaged her brain, you see, so ever since she's been blind and well, she's just gone on growing like this. But we love her, don't we?' Ruth banged her head back against the pram and rocked and made gurgling noises in her throat. Even though the child was blind, speechless and doubly incontinent, there was at that time little support for parents, financial or otherwise. The only recourse would have been to have Ruth 'put away in a home', something her parents wouldn't even consider. Instead, they cared for her unaided twenty-four hours a day, keeping her clean, spoon-feeding her, taking her with them whenever they worked in their fields, talking to her. She replied by grinding her teeth and banging her head back as she rocked, helpless, to and fro. And still, somehow, Julia and George remained cheerful, laughing, joking and generous to a fault.

Entering the kitchen had been a shock and only good manners stopped us showing it. A big fireguard surrounded the fire and on it steamed inadequately washed nappies giving off an aroma, which mingled with various cooking smells.

Julia scooped the washing to one side.

'Sorry about this,' she said. 'It's so hard to get things dry when they have to be washed so often, and we've no hot water, only what we boil from the cold tap in the garden.'

George looked at Julia. 'Oh come, Mother,' he said, 'you can't say we haven't got running water.' He crossed the room and pushed open a door leading out into a small, lean-to scullery at the back. 'Look, our own stream' and he pointed to a trickle of water bubbling happily across the cobblestone floor. 'It gets bigger when it rains.' He grinned. 'One of these days, when I've got time, I'm going fishing in there!'

Julia laughed and began to pour thick tea from a

pot, which had been sitting by the fire. 'Will you have something to eat?' she asked ' I've got bonnag and there's butter there.' She pointed to the table. We hesitated and she went on, 'Bonnag. It's Manx soda bread cooked over the fire on a griddle. Try it.'

'Well, actually,' Mother said hurriedly. 'We left a stew cooking, and it's getting dark, so we'd better not stop, but thanks anyway,' and somehow she swallowed her cup of tea.

On another occasion Mother made some remark about going into town to look for an extra chair for the front room.

'Oh, don't do that,' beamed George. 'We've got a sofa you can have. It's in the other room and we never use it, do we Mother?' Curious, we followed him across the tiny hall and he heaved open the door opposite the kitchen. There, abandoned amid various bags, boxes and sacks of corn, stood a once plush, once pink, two-seater sofa, just visible beneath its dust. Even at a glance we could see springs sagging out through the base.

'Give it a brush,' said Julia, 'and it'll do to be going on with.'

As usual, Mother could find no way of refusing without giving offence, so it was agreed that we'd haul it home – it had castors – on the following Sunday evening. 'Well, you never know,' she said trying to be optimistic as we walked home later, 'it might clean up.'

We were fortunate that it was only half-moon on Sunday so no-one saw us as we half carried, half dragged the dusty object a quarter of a mile back up the road to our house; but we stopped many times, breathless and collapsing in laughter. We heaved it into the front room, but before we'd even shut the front door our cats had sprung into action. They rushed round the room, delighted to be chasing a family of mice who had hitherto lived so peacefully in the webbing beneath the cushions. Shrinking back against the wall in horror, Mother shrieked, 'Quick! Open the back door. Get rid of it!' and the sofa went outside a deal more quickly than it had come in. I can't remember whether it ended on a bonfire or in the garage for the hens to perch on. But that didn't matter. Since our benefactors never visited us, they didn't know what happened, and they would have probably laughed with us if they had.

Chapter 8

'That will do nicely,' said Mother picking up a piece of wood from a fallen tree. It just about came up to my waist and sprouted lots of bare branches. 'We'll paint it white when it's dry. It's not what we're used to but it will do.'

It was mid December in our first year on the island and we were on a Saturday afternoon trawl across damp fields to gather wood for the fire.

'Paint it?' I echoed. 'What for?'

'Christmas,' said Mother. 'We've got to have a Christmas tree and we can't get a real one this year, so we'll make our own. We're not letting Christmas pass without a tree, even if Daddy ...' Her voice trailed away. Then, 'It's a good job some of the decorations arrived in one piece.'

The branches were soon painted white and stuck in a coal bucket half full of soil. With tinsel and a few pre-war baubles hanging from the branches and the bucket hidden beneath a red crepe paper shawl, it looked respectable enough. And a few days later I arrived home from school to find that the front room had a real party air about it. It was festooned with fragile, brightly coloured paper chains, stretching from corner to corner across the ceiling. Over the years as I grew taller, they brushed the top of my head, for Scacafell had low ceilings, but that was preferable to the long sticky flypapers, which graced the room in mid-summer. The final transformation to Christmas came as we dipped evergreen leaves in a brew of Epson Salts and water, which glistened as it dried.

Mother did all she could to make the festive season exciting and normal and every year, poor though we were, we filled a stocking for each other.

She had some strange things in hers – badly knitted kettle-holders to protect her hand from hot handles, candles or matches sneaked from the larder, fir cones to forecast the weather, cheap plaster ornaments. One year she found a small, poorly wrapped flue-brush peeping out of her stocking; another a large cardboard canister of Vim cleaning powder – well, I had to fill the stocking somehow! We maintained the ritual until the Christmas she died, and I'm sure we were both glad that my gifts to her improved!

For her part, she somehow managed to save enough to provide presents – home-made clothes for my dolls, knitted pixie hoods, scarves or mittens for me, once a furry nightdress case in the shape of a dog which, when his tummy was unzipped served as a cosy foot-warmer. I also treasured a golden-haired doll, which Aunty Det sent. I christened her Dorothy after my older cousin. I could brush and curl this doll's hair, which led to the idea of playing hairdressers. Unfortunately both Teddy and Golly were customers too, and for the rest of their lives they both sported a crew cut, which proves that even a bear can spot a fashion long before it becomes popular.

Most toys came and went but books, often the choice of one of the aunts, were always my favourite gifts. Auntie Winnie was especially good at this: Enid Blyton's 'Nature Lovers' Book' (a 1944 red volume of walks through the seasons) and in subsequent years Daily Mail Annuals.

But my favourites were Blyton's 'Josie, Click and Bun' picture books about a doll, a mouse and a rabbit, because I could colour the illustrations (thereby reducing their collectors' value decades later) and a 'Japhet and Happy's Annual'. This was a News Chronicle publication, which was, so the forward notes, '...the second annual to appear under war-time conditions.' Japhet, son of the Noah family of wooden doll-like figures, had first appeared a few months after the First World War in the Chronicle's 'Daily News'. Now, here he was again with his friend, a portly little bear called Happy, both complete with gas-masks, reflecting with a smile the wartime conditions everyone was living in during a Second World War. Needless to say, Japhet now looks out from loose and very tattered pages, for this, with more Enid Blyton books and twelve volumes of Arthur Mee's 'Children's Encyclopaedia' (bought by Daddy 'for Ann when she's older') form physical reminders of the joy I first found in reading.

But it was when I was just nine that I received something I knew I'd always wanted. Mid November and the sound of sawing echoed up the garden from the garage.

'What's he doing?' I asked, for Sid still popped in occasionally to help with minor repairs.

'Just an odd job,' came the unsatisfactory reply. 'Don't go in there and mess things up for him.'

But I was curious and when Mother went up to the shop a few days later, I hauled open the garage door and crept inside. There, under an old sheet, was a half made object, which looked suspiciously as if it could become a doll's cot. Was it? If it was, who was it for? I dare not ask. I could only pray that it might be for me. Christmas: prayer answered. There under a cloth outside the back door on a sunny Christmas morning I found the cot, by then painted a pale green and complete with home made bed linen – and I had to look surprised!

Not every Christmas morning was sunny of course. Occasionally winter would give us frost and a few light snowy days, but that was not very often. Ellan Vannin's climate is temperate and the seasons generally followed a pattern. We were sunburned in the summer, sometimes soaked several times a day in winter and most of the time prevailing winds ensured that we sported wild hairstyles; but like everywhere else, we suffered heavy snowfalls in 1946/7. For most of the time from mid January to mid March Snaefell looked like a giant iced cake, ice formed inside our windows each night and we seemed always to be shivering. On the worst day we woke once more to a strange light and the discovery that snow had stacked itself up almost to the top of the front door. We couldn't see the front gate and there were great drifts in the road.

'Come on then, 'said Mother, coated and Wellington booted. 'We can't stay here all day. Let's see if the shop's open.'

So we shovelled our way out of the house and down the path and out on to what used to be the road, but was now a high, pristine white bank. At long last, glowing with effort, soaking wet and with snow down our wellies, we reached the shop. It was open, but obviously without fresh provisions. It was then that we realised that we'd walked most of the way along the top of the hedge. Our main meal that day was beans on toast.

Winter evenings were always spent with just the two of us in lamplight by the fireside, reading, knitting, sewing, making artificial flowers out of paper or glitter-wax, playing cards and board games or listening to the wireless. So while Ruff dozed at our feet, I learned the intricacies of Whist, Gin Rummy and Strip Jack Naked; played Newmarket for matches and became good at Draughts. Sometimes we used the cards to tell our fortunes, consulting an incredibly fat and dog-eared copy of 'Enquire Within' to unlock the secrets of the future. That was a book like no other, having answers to everything, be it general knowledge, home management, catering, gardening, medical matters or 'starting children in life'. It even had a Ready Reckoner which could tell you, for example, how much you must pay if you bought sixteen items at three-pence three-farthings – (answer: five shillings in 'old money' or twenty-five new pence!) The fire, devouring the logs or dancing through coals, spread a feeling of comfort and well-being that we may not have felt in daylight; and with a 'sausage' of fabric rolled up against the doors to keep the draught out, we were warm in that little front room. And if we had no sweets, we could at least occasionally enjoy spearing the seeds out of a pomegranate with a pin to eat instead.

'Time for the news,' Mother would say and she'd stretch out to switch on the wireless, which sat on a round bamboo table beside her chair.

'This is the Nine O'clock News and this is Alvar Liddell/John Snagge reading it.' Knowing who the broadcaster was, even though we had no idea what he looked like, somehow made him not just a newsreader, but also a friend who was keeping us informed and trying to help us make the best of whatever was happening. Our favourite programmes were those which gave us laughter – like Variety Bandbox, Arthur Askey with his silly songs and of course Tommy Handley's ITMA – 'It's That Man Again'. We knew all the characters and some of their catch phrases became ours: 'lovely grub' (George Gorge); 'I go, I come back' (Ali Oop); 'Can I do you now Sir?' (Mrs Mopp) and of course, the regular sign off 'TTFN (Ta-ta for now). It was this programme, I think, which obliquely set me off into the world of entertainment. After the war, in October 1946, we also became addicted to radio's first daily serial, 'Dick Barton, Special Agent'. This clever but impeccable man (no swearing, sex or booze) with his side-kicks Jock and Snowy got into and out of the most exciting adventures which we just didn't want to miss. But we were only two of his many fans. That serial, broadcast on the Light Programme at 6.45 pm each Monday to Friday for fifteen minutes until March 1951, boasted fifteen million listeners. I'm sure most of them, however old, on hearing its iconic signature tune, 'The Devil's Gallop' are whisked back to family excitement round a radio.

It was during these evenings by the fireside that Mother could sometimes be persuaded to recall happier times when she was a young girl herself.

'We had some funny people come into the bakery,' she would say as she stroked Topsy on her knee. 'I remember one woman who always came in after eleven o'clock. We used to ask her what time it was just to hear her reply. For some reason, it was always 'half past a lemon.' She talked a lot about her Persian cat, too. We had to hear how soft and beautiful his fur was and how it was so thick that she had to brush him every day. 'Well', she would say, 'he's not an ordinary cat, you know. He's half a portion.' A large woman living near the shop was mother to an unruly boy who rarely, if ever, did as he was told. 'Come in here,' she'd roar from the open door as he ran off laughing down the street. 'Alright then! Stay out!' and she'd heave herself back inside, adding before she slammed the door, 'Stay out! I'll have you obey me somehow!' She recalled Esther, who worked as a cleaner in the bake-house, an excellent worker up to a point – or rather a square. Whatever she cleaned, be it window or floor, there would always be one small square which remained unwashed. Even if sent back to do it again, that area would remain untouched. These and many other memories made us laugh together and soon it would be time for bed and rich cocoa, made with water, sugar and a splash of milk, and another day was done.

But it was when I was ill that bedtime became special, for then Mother made a fire in the tiny bedroom grate. It was so comforting to lie snuggled under blankets in the firelight, watching shadows dance and flicker on the walls, while coal-gas popped and ashes whispered as they dropped into the hearth. Dreaming in the glow, I became wrapped in gentle warmth, so that pains faded and I really did 'feel better tomorrow'.

I suffered all the usual childhood ills, most of which had to run their course without medical intervention: measles and chicken pox, coughs and colds and innumerable bouts of tonsilitis. Then, unable to eat solid food, I was treated to bowls of warm bread and milk sweetened with sugar: 'pobs' Mother called it. I don't know where she got the word from, but it comforted me.

We were lucky that the doctor lived only a five-minute walk away. If we really needed and could afford his attention, we visited him in his own home, a double-fronted detached house. A room to the right of the hallway was the waiting room with the surgery behind it. Patients sat on the doctor's dining chairs and gazed at shiny green-patterned lino until he popped out of the consulting room to welcome them in. Occasionally his wife would pass through on some errand from the family side of the house,

'Good morning, how are you?'

'Fine, thank you.' The answer always denied the importance of a visit, but still there was a smile and a chat as if we were visiting friends, which in many cases I suppose we were.

It was this doctor who nursed Mother through a major illness when I was twelve. A cold turned into double pneumonia. She lay in the back bedroom gravely ill, but I suspect had refused to be hospitalised.

'Can you look after her?' He peered at me, then added, 'I'll get Mrs Mylrea to come over and help while you're at school.'

Soon Mother was able to stagger into my double bed and I, with Dr Heny, watched over her. He or the District Nurse visited two or three times day and I was given a variety of tablets to administer. These gathered round Olly on my narrow iron mantle-piece and his beady eyes seemed to watch as they slowly disappeared. Olly was a small brown clock in the shape of an owl, the clock face and mechanism inside the bulge of his stomach. 'Olly says it's time' became a mantra, which charted each day's pill taking and Mother's slow recovery.

It was a frightening episode for both of us, and

even when she was well again Mother had to endure severe asthma attacks for the rest of her life. Damp Scacafell certainly made its mark on her. The Nurse became a friend and she always travelled with her little black Scottie dog in her car. Once when I lay plastered with calamine lotion against the irritations of chicken pox, she held him up outside our gate, so that I could wave to him through the window. The smallest act can sometimes be remembered for a lifetime.

It was in the second year that Mother had to go out to work. The War Widows' pension really wouldn't stretch to everything we needed. The doctor's wife tried to help by offering her the occasional cleaning job, but clearly this would not bring in enough to swell the coffers.

'Well, why not see if you can get something at the woollen mill?' she suggested. 'It's not too far away so you can get back home at dinner time.' That was something Mother always made sure that she did, and although she must have tramped nearly five miles a day back and forth to work, in all weathers, I never arrived home from school to an empty house. She was always there for me.

Penrice's woollen mill was about a mile away, at the foot of Sulby Glen. It was not a large mill but at that time it was quite busy, and in summer woollen cloths of various colours were tented out to dry near the solid building, which backed on to the river. Manx wool was woven into tweeds, including a Manx tartan of pale blue, squared with fine lines of darker blue, green, yellow and white, much of which became travelling rugs. It was one of Mother's jobs to twist the end wools of each rug into fringes, a monotonous, greasy job, which I found impossible to do, but it did help financially. It took all Mother's ingenuity to make ends meet, but she believed and often said, 'Take care of the pennies and the pounds will look after themselves.'

Children are always hungry when they arrive home from school and I was no exception.

'What's for tea?'

'Two jumps at the cupboard door and a bite at the latch.'

Mother concocted all sorts of dishes for every meal, and I grew up well on them.

Breakfast may only have been as simple as porridge or eggy bread pan-fried over the oil stove, beef dripping on toast when we'd been lucky enough to have a small piece of meat, or bread and jam when we'd used up our margarine ration – we never liked Manx butter. We always had a hot dinner every day – though perhaps not 'potatoes, meat and gravy' which was Ethel's unfailing reply to any question as to what she'd had to eat. Stockpot soups and stews (the knuckle bone then a treat for Ruff); tripe boiled with milk and onions or eaten straight from the butcher's with vinegar and bread and margarine; Lancashire hotpot which didn't need too much neck of lamb to be tasty; rabbit stew (with or without butter beans, which were cream coloured and shiny on the outside but soft and floury to eat); bacon and eggs and, of course, corned beef. Sometimes this was just sliced cold, but like thousands of other housewives, Mother became adept at disguising it. She minced, hashed, moulded and frittered it and turned it into rissoles.

Occasionally she proudly bore home half a sheep's head, and to my exclamations of dismay and disgust, replied, 'Just you wait. You'll be surprised. I can make brawn out of this. It's a been a good old English dish since the fifteenth century.' She did make it but it was a long laborious process. The head was boiled, the liquid strained, meat minced and then set in gelatine. By then it looked a pale grey and no more appetising than it had in the beginning, but we ate it with hot mashed potato or cold with bread and pickled beetroot. I was not impressed. I didn't like its gritty taste, and I've never eaten it since.

On the other hand, I enjoyed Yorkshire Pudding. We had five ways of serving that, both savoury and sweet. Sometimes we tried Manx recipes – 'Spuds N' Herrin', for example, a staple in the old Manx diet. For this Herrings were placed on top of partially cooked, part drained potatoes to cook in the steam under a tight-fitting lid, but herrings have many hair-like bones and we didn't get on very well with them. Smoked, they make succulent kippers, and the Manx kipper is the best in the world, but those were so rich that we couldn't eat them too often either. We got on well with the 'Spuds' though. The government's 'Potato Pete' leaflet told us they would '…put a pep in your step' and Pete advised on a variety of uses:

'Potatoes new, Potatoes old,
Potatoes in a salad (cold),
Potatoes baked or mashed or fried,

Potatoes whole, Potatoes pied,

Enjoy them all, including chips,

Remembering spuds don't come in ships.'

Cooked until floury then mashed, they formed the basis for many wartime recipes – scones, cakes, puddings and pastries – and could be used to bulk out other ingredients, such as cheese for Welsh Rarebit. At least we were lucky to have our own eggs. We were not dependent on the adult ration of one egg a week (or every two weeks if in short supply) or powdered egg – so we never had to welcome advice on how to hard-boil dried eggs!

'Eat well and keep warm, and you won't go far wrong,' said Mother and she battled on with next to nothing and no help in the equipment she had to use.

Sometimes she noted down useful recipes in indelible pencil. They are still there in a pre-war notebook, which she had used as a confectioner in the bake-house. Between recipes for Christmas Cake (17lb dried fruit, 7lb eggs, 6lb Barbados sugar, ½ pint brandy…) and Confectioner's Custard (4 quarts fresh milk, 32 eggs, 3lb sugar…) are instructions for 'wartime pudding'. She had written, 'Take ¼ lb each of flour, sugar, breadcrumbs, currants, add one egg and a medium size carrot, grated …'

In the same book she also jotted down wartime recipes for Malt Loaf using Ovaltine, and Chocolate Spread made from cocoa and custard powder, boiled with milk, a little butter and sugar until thick. In my mother's recipe book I had pencilled in the one-word comment 'Delisous'!

Some ingredients remained scarce long after the war. In a recipe from the late 40s, a lemon had been augmented with apples to make Lemon Curd. Beside it is a scribbled note, 'doesn't keep very long'.

She taught me how to knead dough, and while she 'knocked up' loaves, I made bread rolls that looked like plaits – and the kitchen smelt wonderful. I should still practise those skills, but regrettably I don't. Times have changed.

Chapter 9

*G*radually life began to form a pattern and yet again it was Saturday. For once Tuesday's pension had lasted long enough for us to take an extra trip into town. It was to be a treat so that we could wander round without concentrating only on shopping –'Tea, butter, sugar, marg, lard …'. Every time we wrote a shopping list that was how it started and for the rest of my life, without thinking, my shopping lists still begin that way!

This time we travelled lazily, by Joe's bus. We were not alone in preferring this independent, friendly, one-man service to the usual transport. Joe was happy and obliging and his bus stops were, within reason, wherever you wanted them to be – ours was outside Maggie's shop. He had a typical Manx traa-de-looar outlook on life and nobody ever minded if he was a few minutes late. We knew he'd arrive eventually. Always willing to deliver medicine, parcels or newspapers along the route, his cheerful demeanour was echoed by two illustrated postcards, which he had stuck behind his interior driving mirror. The first read

'Step along gaily; the trouble in front isn't there.'
And the second

'Never trouble trouble till trouble troubles you,

Or you'll make a double trouble and trouble others too.'
One doesn't often enjoy a journey which comes with such free and memorable advice.

'Here we are then, folks, Royal Ramsey,' Joe smiled as he turned into Parliament Square and we all piled out of his old bus. 'See you later.'

Royal Ramsey. At school I'd learned that the royal title derived from a visit made in 1847 by Queen Victoria – or rather a visit not made, for she did not set foot on Manx soil. As happens so often that it is a fact as much as Manx legend, when Royalty approaches the island, the Celtic sea-god, Mannanan Mac Lir is seen to cast storms, or shroud the island coasts in an almost impenetrable mist. In 1847, the seas raged so fiercely that the Royal ship could not land at Douglas, but was forced to divert to Ramsey instead. Prince Albert braved the elements – there's a tower on Lhergy Frissel hill above the town commemorating his visit – but the Queen, suffering severe sea-sickness, lay prone on board ship. As one who travelled across the Irish Sea, she had my sympathy.

Before we set off along Parliament Street, we turned to a tiny sweetshop in a corner of the Square, which we always visited when we still had enough coupons for our monthly twelve-ounce ration of sweets. It was tucked in an angle between the meeting of two roads so that it appeared triangular, like an upended Toblerone. I saved up for Crunchie Bars, but Mother could never have the sticky pre-war Pontefract Cakes she loved. Ration spent, we made do with chlorodyne cough sweets or little packs of Horlicks tablets for which we didn't need coupons. But that day the shop was shut and only fat, empty pre-war jars stood in the window. Never mind, perhaps next time...

As we arrived at the quay to visit an agricultural merchant to buy mash for the hens, we stopped to look at the fishing boats, and it was here that we first came across some of the many superstitions, which are so much part of the Isle of Man.

'What's he doing?' I asked as we watched an old fisherman scrabbling through piles of net on a fishing boat. He was picking out small white stones caught in the nets and tossing them into the harbour.

'Do you not know, girlie?' said another old man leaning on a rail nearby. 'Them's clagh bane.' He examined his pipe before clamping it more firmly between his gums. 'Clagh bane. Stones o' the dead. In the old days white stones like them covered graves. It'd be unlucky to have any o' them aboard.' He puffed and spat. 'And when them fishin' boats'll go out,' he continued, 'D'you know why they'll not all follow each other in a line?'

'What do you mean?' Mother took up the conversation.

'Well, first boat'll lead,' he said, 'then the next two'll go together, side by side. Can have no third boat, 'tis unlucky.' He gazed into the distance, and since the conversation appeared to be over, we turned away. Then he called, 'And if you want to put a sight on ben varrey, girlie,' he tutted at our obvious ignorance, 'woman of the sea – mermaid to you – go to Peel. They're there.' For a long time we wondered about Manx mermaids, but when we eventually saw seals basking on seaside rocks at Peel, we believed we'd solved the mystery.

'Can't we go over the swing bridge to see the park?' I coaxed, as we arrived at the point where the Sulby meets the sea. 'Just for a little way, we needn't go in.'

Mother considered for a moment. 'Alright,' she said, obviously as curious about the Mooragh as I was.

We'd been visiting Ramsey in safety for a year now and knew most of it, except for Daddy's forbidden zone on the north promenade. 'But we'll go the back way, then we won't pass the internment camp.'

So we made a detour and by walking up shady, tree-lined paths on higher ground behind our destination, we were able look down into Mooragh Park. Below us, paths edged with palm trees and fresh green lawns surrounded a lake with a small island in the middle. Beyond the park we could see a narrow, miniature golf course and the promenade. The whole area was fenced in by a double ring of barbed wire, as were the tall boarding houses edging the far side of the park. Beyond the promenade, waves rippled freely on

Mooragh Park, Ramsey, 1950s

to the shore. A few prisoners wandered round in a desultory fashion, some throwing a ball, and then we noticed a single figure running, running as if possessed. Dishevelled and sweating, clad in trousers and grey vest, he was running round and round inside the perimeter fence, seeing no-one, speaking to no-one. Even as a child, I felt a sense of shock. I'd been to the zoo, seen animals in cages, but had never seen a man behind wire – not that he was really caged, for the park covers a large area, but he'd lost his freedom, that much was evident.

'That's enough. We've seen it now,' said Mother sharply. 'Come on, we've things to do.' And the Mooragh remained out of bounds to us until long after 2nd August 1945 when the camp, by then one of only two left on the island, finally closed.

But Mother would never have sanctioned the visit

in the first place had she known that three months earlier there had been violence there. Finns, Italians and Germans, all segregated and under the eye of sentries and armed guards, were housed in the boarding houses. Some caused trouble, but none of them were considered to be dangerous 'Category A' prisoners (they were mainly imprisoned in Peel). However, here in Ramsey, trouble had been escalating since it was known that pro-Nazis planned to celebrate Hitler's birthday on 20th April. There'd been arguments and looting and the Finns, in particular, were known to be quarrelsome. Just after midday on that April day one of them, a young man of twenty-six, carefully walked across to house No 9 where another Finn was standing, and threw a bucket of dirty water over him. The reaction was swift. Before the guards could intervene, there was a fight and the attacker lay dead on the pavement, stabbed in the stomach with a sharpened kitchen knife. The murderer was proven not guilty on a plea of provocation, but the incident had provided a ripple of local interest, which we had missed.

On the whole, this camp was a peaceful place and in time some of the men worked for local farmers, replacing the Manx who had left to serve in the forces. The camps also provided work and revenue for local people. Government rent for requisitioned houses replaced lost tourist revenue and the extra administration needed to serve the camp provided jobs. At its busiest, food for the Mooragh alone included a daily supply of 40 gallons of milk and 500 lbs of bread, with

240 lbs of meat, sugar and jam as well as all the necessary potatoes and vegetables. The camp commander was also able to use his discretion in allowing some newspapers to be brought in and a few radio broadcasts to be received. Little wonder that in all its five years, there were only two attempts to escape from the Mooragh.

Having retraced our steps rather hurriedly we arrived back on the Quay and went to buy the hen food. The merchant's premises, housing farmers' equipment, grains and bags of coal seemed large and very dusty. As Mother bought the mash, I noticed a kitten curled up in a tight ball on a bag of grain. Her fur was a pale patchwork of browns and yellows, but she was very thin. She looked up at me with sad, tired eyes and stretched and it was then that I noticed she looked different. 'Look,' I called to Mother, who was moving to the door. 'This cat hasn't got a tail.'

The corn merchant strolled over. ' She's a rumpy,' he said, 'not a true Manx cat. They don't have any tail at all, and the back legs are long like a hare. It's the way they're born.' So much for tales about Noah shutting the Ark just as the Manx cat was entering. 'But this one's got a stump, see?' He picked the cat up roughly and pointed to a little bump where her tail should be. 'See, a rumpy. You can have her if you like. Don't know where she came from, but I don't want her here.' So Torty joined the family (an obvious name, since she was tortoiseshell coloured and her name had to begin with T to complement Topsy and Tico.)

We acquired many cats over the years, though the

order of their coming and our partings are sketchy. Memory only recalls their personalities, the love they gave and the fun we had with them. As kittens they gazed in terror at their reflections in a long mirror set at floor level against a wall; tied themselves in knots chasing a ball of wool; rushed round the house after ping-pong balls or tried to jump over the low bar under the sideboard without moving their front paws. 'Oor Wullie', black and white and named after a Scottish character in a comic, used to rush up the back of the settee or the curtains wild-eyed, tail lashing, for no other reason than he felt like it. Clancy liked to 'lower the boom' to quote a song of the time. He was a thin, white cat, who enjoyed bringing down an out-stretched paw on the head of any unsuspecting feline who happened to pass by. Mr Jinna, on the other hand, was a ginger Persian, proud and haughty, his colour and regal bearing leading him to be called Mr Jinna after the Prime Minister of India. He always ran out to meet Mother when he heard her footsteps on the lane, but he did this once too often and ran straight into a car.

We loved our cats and they paid their way by keeping down the mouse and rat population in Scacafell's garden. They shared our food and had a weekly supply of cooked 'pluck' (lungs), bright red and soft and possibly the only bit of offal that people didn't eat in wartime. In fact, I think word spread into the feline world that in our house all would be made welcome if there was no fighting. I don't remember any, even though at one time I think we actually had seven furry friends in residence.

Ruff viewed them all with equanimity. He was a dog with an expansive personality and a laissez-faire outlook – unless he met a rat, which was quickly dispatched to rat heaven with a quick toss over one shoulder. After all, didn't this new and delightful countryside belong to him now, in spite of family attempts to keep him in the garden? Didn't most of the traffic go round him when he was dozing in the sun in the middle of the road? When he did wander, Ruff made the most of it, sometimes returning with a young rabbit as a peace offering. Once, in high summer, he returned with his fur reeking with the most unimaginable stomach-turning smell. He padded cheerfully into the kitchen.

'Wherever have you been? Oh, you stink to high heaven!' Ignoring his happy face, Mother thrust him back outside again, snapping at me, 'Kettle's hot. Fill the old tub with water – bring soap and that old towel.' Half an hour later, thoroughly soaped, disinfected and rinsed, Ruff shook water all over us. Then dried, he sat in the sun to lick his paws.

'He must've been in some farmer's midden,' Mother observed. 'Keep an eye on him. Dogs are devils for muck.' But dreams of his adventure kept Ruff happily snoozing by the back door till bedtime. The performance was repeated on the next afternoon, and again on the following day and each time he returned, his panting grin seemed to get wider. The mud which covered him was brown, rank and sticky. For the rest of the week he was not allowed out unaccompanied and holes in the hedges were reinforced with old tea trays, bits of wood and anything we could lay our hands on.

'Your dog been over the fields into that stinking muck?' Ethel's father asked and when we said he had, he went on, 'So's our dog. I'll sort it.' He eventually solved the mystery and rectified it. In a field some distance away, a local farmer had inadequately buried the rotting corpse of a horse. What heaven it must have been to roll in! Why do some dogs believe that clean fur should be made muddy and smelly whenever and wherever possible?

There were, on occasions, creatures we didn't welcome like the goats and here I also include a plague of much smaller creatures, which attacked me one summer's day in the back garden. I'd wandered down the dividing hedge between Ethel's garden and our own. At that time they kept pigs and they obviously needed cleaning out.

'I wouldn't come over here,' I called to Mother, 'The pigs stink.' Then turning away, I looked down. 'Ugh! My slippers!' I snatched off my red slippers, now boasting fine black trimming which was moving, jumping. 'Fleas! Oh! Help!'

That day I quickly found that there are two ways of disposing of fleas without insecticide. They can be plunged into water to swim round frantically until they drown, or snatched up between finger and thumb and pressed between two thumb nails, a quicker death, but slower to execute. Outraged, since she was so careful to smother our pets periodically with flea powder, Mother 'had a word' with our neighbour and this never happened again; but I had inadvertently learned an extra curricular skill which I'd never expected to acquire.

But it was not only summer-time which taught us much about country life. One winter's night, as we were about to go to bed, we heard above the trees tossing in the wind, an eerie bumping and thumping in the garden outside.

'What's that?' Together we listened, wide-eyed and frozen. 'It's coming nearer,' Mother whispered. And it was. The bumping seemed to approach the low window of the front room where we stood. Did we imagine the snuffle of heavy breathing? There was definitely a presence out there in the cold darkness, just the other side of the house wall. There it was again, a muffled, trampling sound, moving, it seemed, across the front garden. We dare not lift the blind to peer out of the window for fear of what might be gazing through the glass. We dare not open the door. Outside there was pitch darkness and a restless wind – no street lights, no electricity, no telephone for half a mile.

'I'm not going to bed,' said Mother. ' You never know …'

She turned up the wick on the lamp again, stoked up the fire against the kettle and then crept into the kitchen to fetch the cocoa tin and milk. We sat together by the fireside sipping cocoa and whispering. There was nothing else we could do but stay quiet and hope 'it' would go away, then wait until daylight when we could see what was going on. After about an hour, everything seemed quiet again.

'Well, we can't sit up all night,' murmured Mother. 'If we get no sleep we'll look like bog-eyed twirls tomorrow.' She did have some funny turns of phrase. 'Come on, and we'll share my bed in the back room. At least it can't get in.' But she didn't sound too sure.

Next morning we crept into the front room and Mother gingerly pulled up the corner of the blind. Then she let it fly up with a bang and started to laugh.

'Oh, just look! Look at that!' she exclaimed.

I shot over to the window and there, lying comfortably in our front garden against the house wall were three great black and white cows, stolidly chewing the cud and blinking in the early light. Escaping from their field down the road, they'd wandered through our open gate and after bumbling round in the dark had settled down for the night. An apologetic farmer arrived to collect the beasts but it was some time before the garden recovered from our nocturnal visitors.

'Oh, well, that's country life, I suppose,' Mother remarked philosophically and went to coax the kitchen fire into flame so that we could have breakfast.

Chapter 10

As it always does, spring brought a new lease of life and I loved the sense of freedom that came with it after a buttoned up winter. Now we could walk the dog without seeing his ears blow inside out as we leaned against eye-wateringly cold winds. Instead, with my new friends, generally Jean and her sister Dorothy, I explored our village further and discovered fresh beauty in the Manx countryside. We found where the first violets and wide-eyed primroses peeped in the hedges, and Mother always received spring's first sweet-smelling posy to put by the photograph. We came home with arms full of daffodils which grew profusely in the corner of a field, deep yellow, double-petalled blossoms, bursting with that special pollen smell which naturally grown daffodils have. We gathered hands full of bluebells and fine-stemmed, pink 'milk-maids' (lady smock), celandines, delicate white stitchwort and wood anemones, meadow vetch and blue-washed speedwell, jamming them all into various jars so that we could admire their beauty. Later we wandered freely over distant, damp unused pastures and knelt to pick wild marsh orchids, pink and white and purple, always leaving some, but never dreaming that we were culling flowers which were to become so rare. In summer we gathered Queen of the Meadow, long stems of feathery Meadowsweet, and breathed in the heady, honey perfume of its creamy white fronds; then back at Scacafell, saw Mr Caine digging in his garden. He leaned on his spade and shook his head.

'Leave that outside now,' he said. 'Don't go putting that in your bedroom, girl. If you go to sleep with it, you'll never wake up, you know. It's the smell, you see.'

So instead of walking on hard pavements past rows of houses, listening for and learning to identify enemy aircraft as well as our own, I gained an altogether healthier knowledge of life and the countryside, including the local bird life, which shared our wanderings.

'That's a curlew,' said Jean as a plaintive 'coor-lee, coorlee' sounded over the meadows.

'And that's a corncrake' I said later in answer to a harsh 'crekcrek' echoing over the marshes of another field. I was not to be outdone. I knew my birds!

I learned to recognise a Robin's song and the warning call he made, which sounded as if he were winding a watch. I knew a Blackbird when I heard him and checked the Thrush's call against the words he seemed to say, in a verse old Mr Caine had taught me:

'Big Robin, big Robin,

Take a smoke, take a smoke, take smoke,

I have no smoke, I have no smoke,

Buy, buy, buy.

I have not a penny, I have not a penny, I have not
a penny.

Go on trust, go on trust, go on trust.'

And then it was the Easter holidays and we still had May Day to look forward to, when we'd dress up and parade round as May Queens for the day.

'I know,' said Jean, 'tomorrow, let's go up Primrose Hill and roll eggs. I can't on Sunday 'cos it's Church.' Jean's family were staunch Methodist. 'We'll get a bottle at Tommy Pop's and we can have a picnic.' Tommy owned a tiny shop at the far end of the Straight, beyond Sulby Bridge, and although he was round in stature, he earned his name because his stock mainly consisted of bright red and green fizzy pop, dandelion and burdock, lemonade and romantic sounding American cream soda.

On Easter Saturday afternoon, clutching our picnic and hard-boiled eggs, we set off to climb the small hill which overlooked Sulby Claddagh. Yn Claddagh, common land with the river and a road running through it, became our playground in good weather. The ground formed grassy bumps and hollows, great for hide and seek or an obstacle course for a bicycle, and at one end stood Primrose Hill, or Cronk

Cronk Sumark, with the Claddagh at its feet, in spite of its history, a fine playground.

Sumark to give it its official Celtic name. It stands about 250ft high, the climb to the top is steep in places and on one side it appears to have had a bite taken out of the summit. It has since been officially designated an Iron Age Hill Fort, but to us it was just a convenient place to scamper about and have fun. We rolled eggs down through the short grass and bracken near the bottom, rolled after them, screaming and laughing, then climbed to the top to view the countryside before starting all over again.

On the Claddagh below, set back against a hedge, there was an old stone cottage. It looked grey and deserted. I was curious and peeped in through the un-curtained window. All I could see was an earthen floor and a few sticks of furniture.

'Oh, come away!' Jean clutched my arm and pulled me back. 'Cecil will get you. He's scary and dirty. He's got awful, red-rimmed eyes, and he'll shout if he sees us.' Dorothy, older and wiser, laughed.

'Don't be daft. He's just old and he's not all there.' She turned to me. 'Someone gave him a vacuum flask one day, like Dad uses to keep his tea warm, and d'you know what Cecil did?' She giggled. 'He put tea and cold water in it and he was ever so cross when it didn't heat up!'

Cecil, who gesticulated wildly if anyone came near his area of the Claddagh, was only one of the colourful characters who made village life so interesting. Locals knew that pub-lover Jimmy would order a drink from the far end of the Bar so that he could reach across to help himself to cigarette packets at his end; poacher Teddy tried not to get caught until the last week of December so that he'd be sure of his Christmas dinner 'inside' and a set of clothes to start off the new year. We used to count the rhythm of old Chrissie's legs as she cycled past on her ancient sit up and beg bike, and were disappointed if she missed her usual 1-2-3-stop pattern of movement; and when she wore her old raincoat over a new cream mackintosh we knew it was going to rain. They, and the farmer who often trundled to the shop on his tractor to collect his newspaper, unknowingly enriched our lives.

Sometimes we climbed away from the hill, up the Ballamanaugh Road and into fields beyond, where the sisters introduced me to the joys of pulling up a turnip to gnaw at when we were hungry – a change from eating blackberries or the new spring leaves of hawthorn. It was when the hawthorn was in flower that we searched out the Ash tree. 'Come on, we've got to find the lucky leaves,' Jean called as she slithered down a slope to an Ash growing near the bottom.

'Lucky leaves?' I slithered after her.

'Yes. You've got to find a spray with an even number of leaves, not counting the top one, and that'll bring you good luck.'

When the weather was warm, Jean and I went down to the river to paddle and skim stones, or balance our way across slippery rocks at the top of its shallow weir; and all the time we gossiped, giggled and shared 'best friend' secrets.

'Guess what I'm getting for my birthday,' I said as my tenth birthday approached, and before Jean could answer, 'A bike!'

It was very much second hand, re-painted with thick black paint, which bubbled in places and smelled of tar. At first I frequently fell off, but we didn't care. Now, when the sisters could persuade their brothers to lend us one of theirs, we had two bikes between us. At last we could go further afield, two taking it in turns to ride while the other one trotted along at their side.

The preferred destination was Jurby beach, beyond the aerodrome and more than five miles away. Then one day, when we were half way there, Dorothy peered over her glasses and said, 'Oh, I don't want to go any further. I want to read.' So Jean and I, promising to be back soon, left her sitting happily near 'the plantation', in a meadow of soft cotton grass – Ducks' Down or Clooie Hunnug – while we pedalled on to the beach. It was lovely there, soft sand trickling down from sharp marron grass banks, the waves sparkling in the sunlight. We played and paddled, forgot the time and found when we finally left the beach, that Dorothy had become tired of waiting for us and had walked the two or three miles home on her own. So we happily played our young lives away, especially during the summer holidays.

Holidays, in the 1940s, just meant time away from school. By 1945 Mother and I had put down roots and couldn't afford to go 'across' anyway, and perhaps, subconsciously, we were becoming like the Islanders. For generations they had never felt the need to leave the island. They had all they needed there within its 227 square miles. Why bother to venture further? Time enough for that. For us, life was centred in the village and my circle of friends grew – just girls, boys were tolerated only in school. These were easygoing friendships and we had fun. As well as Ethel, Jean and Dorothy, there was Gladys whose father and uncle owned the flour mill; Barbara from the Police Station; Daisy who lived up the Glen, and Florence, an amiable friend known as 'Flokka'. Occasionally I was allowed to go and play with Marion, a quiet girl who lived over a mile away, beyond Sulby Bridge. One attraction there was her playhouse in the garden. It was a small, old-fashioned caravan set at the top of a slope beneath frothy-blossomed apple trees. It smelled of warm wood, dust and vague perfumes, floral curtains covered its tiny windows. Everything was in miniature, even the teacups and the little cakes we had for tea. When we played there we became enveloped in a secret, cosy world. Then suddenly, Marion would announce, 'I'm going in now,' and she'd disappear into the house, leaving me to drift sadly down the three little steps and make my way home.

An altogether more down to earth girl was Eunice. Like me, she was a 'come-over'. She and her family arrived in the village just before we did, and we heard that their coming had caused some amusement. They had arrived on a hot summer's day wearing raincoats and Wellington boots, because some wag had told them that waves washed right over the Steam Packet boats (as in fact they did in winter). They lived in a white house at the corner of our road, near the pub. They had no family connection with RAF Jurby as far as we knew, but Peggy, Eunice's glamorous elder sister, seemed to attract uniforms. One day Eunice arrived back from school earlier than expected. As I continued on my way home, I heard a scream,

'Get out! I told you to stay out …' and turning saw Eunice rush back out on to the pavement followed by her irate sister, blouse flapping, wielding a bread knife. Sadly, when she was eleven Eunice, a coat over her head against rain, ran out of the house to go across to the shop and ended her life in collision with a car. Everyone in the village was stunned. Things like that just didn't happen in Sulby.

If I wasn't pottering round the garden with the doll's pram talking to myself, or sitting by the low kitchen window with Rosie, pretending to be on a train, I'd be playing outside with these friends – no television or video games then. 'Let's play House' or

'Shop'. Various stones, grasses and flowers represented vegetables: holding a sod of turf, we'd ask, 'Would you like your lettuce filleted?' Sometimes we were 'Nurses'. Then I'd copy Auntie Winnie's uniform – home made white apron, nurse's cap a white square folded so as to fan out at the back of the head. Sometimes, with a rope across the road we skipped, in unison – 'All in together girls, never mind the weather girls' and individually – 'Teddy Bear, Teddy Bear, touch the ground…'. We whipped tops, which we'd coloured with chalks, bounced balls in a variety of games. We played marbles, hop-scotch, Nuts in May, Grandmother's footsteps. Clenagh Road saw them all in their season and we just stood aside when a car appeared. We were never bored. Sometimes we might make an obstacle course over the bumps which formed our back garden, and when Ethel and I were in artistic mood we entertained the others with a concert.

A sheet tossed over string across the kitchen became a theatrical curtain. While Ethel and I prepared the stage on one side of it, our audience trooped in to sit seriously and silently on the other side, contemplating what was to come. Mother, I later discovered, could never trust herself to be part of the audience, so she sat in the front room listening and wiping away tears of laughter. The ad hoc entertainment generally began with sketches we'd heard on ITMA: while Ethel played Tommy Handley, I was everyone else. All the characters and their sayings were there in our kitchen, along with puns, quick fire gags we'd heard on the wireless and occasionally

Arthur Askey's 'Busy Bee' song. Sometimes we re-told Fairy Tales.

'Let's do Cinderella this time.' That always went down well. While I swept away imaginary ashes, Ethel doubled as the Ugly Sisters, the Fairy Godmother and a somewhat sheepish Prince – she was not a romantic, though she was good at jokes and tricks. There was rarely an occasion when the programme didn't include my unaccompanied singing and tap-dancing to the first verse, at least, of 'The Sailor with the Navy-blue Eyes' –

'Who's got girls in every port

Hangin' around like flies?

Yo ho ho ho ho ho –o

The sailor with the navy blue eyes'!

I have no idea now what the tune was. The performances generally ended with a drink for all – violent coloured 'pop', or lemonade made with lemon crystals, and if we were lucky a biscuit.

When I joined the Girls Friendly Society, a happy, world-wide, church-based organisation, (my membership destined to help save my life when seriously ill in my early twenties) Ethel and I were able to play out our dramas in a more public way. The GFS met weekly in St Stephen's Church Hall and the first real play I was in, when eleven, was 'The Princess (Jean) and the Woodcutter' (me) by A.A.Milne. Ethel played the Queen and Dorothy was King. Mrs Gale, a peripatetic teacher at Sulby School produced it and it was very successful, although the drama was enhanced during one performance when Ethel leaned back on her throne and fell backwards off the stage. I think I was the only

The author's first taste of drama, with to her left Ethel, Dorothy and Jean.

member of the cast who acquired a life-long love of theatre. I also became involved in the island's GFS competitions, from handwriting, needlework or reading aloud, to choral singing and keep-fit. The competitions were held at the Villa Marina ballroom in Douglas, (where I generally descended from the coach a pale green, either from the journey or nerves) and Sulby won the Keep Fit shield twice. But as a competitor in Reading Aloud I wondered why titters greeted a previously unseen passage, which I was reading with great confidence. I was mortified when I realised that I'd made the mistake of pronouncing 'quay' as 'kway'.

'Oh, words are like that,' laughed Mother when I

told her. 'I remember when I was a little girl I was sent to get some cough mixture and I had to memorise the ingredients. I said them all the way to the chemist's, then when I got there I could only remember ipecacuanha wine, – such a funny word – and one of the others – and that came out wrong. Instead of syrup of squills, whatever that was, I said syrup of squirrels!' She laughed again, and turned back to the job in hand; and while we both pondered on the mysteries of the English language, she beat a rug hanging over the washing line with a bamboo carpet-beater shaped like a three-leaved clover.

Sometimes there were official village entertainments held either in the Chapel Room by the station, where perhaps the night before we had queued to collect new ration books, or in the Church Hall. This might be a Cruinniaght, a music and speech festival, for the Manx are a musical race. I only once had the courage to sing solo, and heard a kindly judge comment on 'a sweet voice, which should be trained'. There were Beetle Drives, Concerts and regular Harvest suppers or Mheilleas ('Melyas') so called after the doll once traditionally made of stalks from the final harvest sheaf. In later years Mother regularly went to Whist Drives. These events, noisy and friendly, were held in the steamy atmosphere of the Hall heated by a stove, where we sat crammed on hard benches to eat strange paste sandwiches and oddly shaped cakes.

So although the adults knew very well that there was a world war bringing terror to those across the water, these fears passed over our young heads. Our only real contribution to the war effort was to try to take sixpence to school on Monday mornings, to buy a National Savings stamp. We grew up believing that carrots helped us to see in the dark, that 'Coughs and Sneezes Spread Diseases' and that a ferocious pear-shaped Squander Bug glaring down at us from posters, dared us to commit the crime of waste. I was extremely lucky that Ellan Vannin gave me the chance to enjoy a relatively normal childhood even though there was a war on. If I had stopped to think, a flower by a photograph would have reminded me how that had come about.

Mother and I became closer as I grew up, and we had many laughs together. Occasionally we ventured away from Sulby, especially as I grew older.

'Tomorrow, we'll go to Douglas. I want to see if I can get any wool in the market,' she might say. Douglas market, not far from the quayside, was inside what to me seemed an ill-lit, overgrown shed. There we'd find a jumble of stalls selling second-hand crockery, clothes and 'antiques', and sometimes vegetables and fish. But I always made a beeline for one corner where they sold old books and magazines. There, for sixpence, I generally acquired a bundle of second hand comics to take home. Then, before catching the train back, we might stop at our favourite chip-smelling café at the end of Strand Street for a cup of tea with a pasty and beans, or some toast. On one occasion we found the place closed.

'Well, I'm dying for a drink,' Mother said as we wandered on up the street, 'so for once we'll go in here.'

'Here' proved to be an up-market establishment where in one corner a palm tree overhung a pianist quietly playing a grand piano, while diners at white-clothed tables were served by heavy-footed waitresses in black. Undaunted, we found a table, ordered tea and cakes and tried to look as if we were at home in such a hallowed atmosphere. Then just as we were finishing tea, I hiccupped. It came forth loudly and unexpectedly from somewhere deep inside. Heads turned and there followed a sudden silence, shattered by yet another hiccup and barely controlled giggles from Mother and me. We were forced to make a sudden and undignified exit so that we could explode into laughter outside this place of politely tinkling teacups.

After two or three years Mother built a regular weekly outing into our 'always busy' routine. Somehow she juggled the finances so that on most Saturday evenings we could go to the 'the pictures' in Ramsey. There were two showings each evening, Monday to Saturday, with a change of programme midweek, but we only ever went to the first house on Saturdays. We had the choice of the Cinema near the 'Toblerone' shop, or the larger Plaza at the other end of town where, I was to discover in my teens, the back row was conveniently furnished with double seats! Every Saturday we dressed up – Mother was determined to keep up our standards. I graduated from a straw sunbonnet or a knitted pixie hood to wearing a 'proper' hat when I was older. My favourite was a light brown felt with an upstanding heart-shaped brim framing my face, a typical late 1940s hat. Whatever the weather, we sallied forth in our best to board the 5.30pm train to Ramsey, the scent of Midnight in Paris or Californian Poppy generally drifting in our wake.

'Can't we have the Violet scent for a change?' I asked once, finding it in Mother's bedroom.

'No', she said, hastily thrusting it in a drawer, 'the bottle's empty. I meant to put it away.' Then I remembered when Daddy had bought her the scent and understood why she wasn't going to share it.

It happened at the beginning of the war, when we were supposed to visit Auntie Connie. Daddy came home from the fire station to say apologetically,

' Sorry, Pops, my shift's been changed, so I can't go, but I'll take you both into Stockport for an hour instead. I've got enough petrol left. You can buy some of that violet scent you wanted.'

There was a scramble to get ready and Mother and I packed into the bullet shaped sidecar of Daddy's pride and joy, his Royal Enfield motorbike. He stopped near the shops and I stood beside him on the pavement while we waited for Mother to join us. But she didn't. She shrank back in the seat, looking embarrassed and cross at the same time.

'What's wrong?' Daddy leaned forward anxiously.

'I can't get out,' Mother said at last, tight lipped. 'We'll have to go home. I can't get out, I've still got my slippers on'.

We looked down at her bedroom slippers and Daddy laughed out loud.

'Oh, you won't want to be seen in those, will you, Pops?' he said and laughed again. 'Well, my dear, you'll have to wait there and Ann and I will go and buy the scent for you. That'll teach you!'

So we'd run hand in hand to the shop to choose a pretty little wicker covered bottle of perfume, which he knew she wanted. It was in a violet covered box and years later, there it was, just as when it was bought, a precious reminder of happier times.

During our picture-going days we enjoyed a wide variety of films – U and A certificate, B movies, lavish Hollywood Musicals and classics. Old Mother Riley, Laurel and Hardy, Abbot and Costello, The Three Stooges, whatever it was, the magic of cinema took us away from the realities of life. But inevitably there was, too, that white cockerel flapping its wings and crowing to announce Pathe News.

The newsreels bothered me. There was always, it seemed, against a background of suitably stirring music, footage of 'our brave boys at the Front' winning battles, fighting for their families and the glory that was Britain, and all to often the Royal Air Force figured in these reports. It was then that I had to create a diversion. I'd drop a coin, pretend pins and needles, lose my gloves on the floor, anything to take Mother's attention away from the screen. I didn't want her upset by the sight of blue-uniformed or flying-suited airmen flying off, perhaps never to return. My concern was unspoken and I don't know if she was ever aware of what I was trying to do. If she was, she never said so, but foolishly I felt that I had to protect her from the pain of memory. The film over, we'd return for the 8.30 train by way of the chip shop.

'Fish and chips for two, please, with salt and vinegar.' The hot, fragrant, newspaper-wrapped parcel was borne home in triumph, and only occasionally was I allowed to steal a chip to taste before we got home. Supper was always reheated in the oil-stove oven to be eaten 'properly' from a plate at the table. Standards were never allowed to slip.

Chapter 11

*I*t was 1945. 'Two prisoners have escaped from the Mooragh!' Jean, eyes wide, greeted me at her front door one Saturday afternoon in early March. 'There're hundreds of people looking for them.'

Everyone in the village was wondering how the men had managed to get away, and if they'd put to sea, like three others had done in 1941. Then they had cut through the wire on a stormy night, stolen a boat to sail west, been driven east by gale-force winds, recaptured and sent to a camp in Peel. Since it seemed now that the war would soon be over, people wondered why these last prisoners had even bothered to try. There were only two men's internment camps left on the island. As dusk fell, Jean and I clutched each other fearfully as we ran up and down the Straight, 'seeing each other home' as usual, but we needn't have worried. On a crisp Sunday morning, after only a week of freedom, two thoroughly demoralised, weary men walked into Bride Post Office four miles away from their camp, and about six as the crow flies from us, to give themselves up. Apparently they had known they would never make a complete escape, but frustrated at being refused repatriation, had wanted to make a gesture. They had slept rough and never been a threat to anyone. On 2nd August, nearly three months after VE Day, their camp at the Mooragh closed, and during the first week in September the last 580 prisoners on the Island left for Fleetwood.

Like the rest of the British Isles, the island celebrated VE Day on 8th May. Church bells, silent for years, rang out; parties were organised in flag bedecked streets; bonfires appeared on beaches and fireworks, which had been hoarded for just such an occasion, decorated the sky. Everyone was in holiday mood in spite of drizzly weather and there were no letters delivered for two days because the postmen took time off. And amid all the celebration there was more news guaranteed to cause great excitement. On Wednesday 4th July King George VI and Queen Elizabeth were to make a three day visit to the island, the first visit they had been able to make outside Great Britain since war began. They were to attend the ceremony of Tynwald on the 5th July, the Island's national day. This would be a truly historic occasion, for this was the first time a King and Queen had been present at the reading of the laws on Tynwald Hill in St Johns.

'Oh, we'll read all about it in The Courier,' said Mother. 'Everywhere will be packed and we wouldn't see anything even if we went to Ramsey to see them.' She was right. The local paper showed Parliament Square as a sea of people milling beneath acres of flags just as they had done in May.

So in Scacafell life continued as usual in spite of the royal presence. On the Friday, a school holiday to celebrate Tynwald, I donned my coat and wellingtons and set off across the fields to gather wood – the fire had to be lit every day, come what may. Arriving back at the field gate facing our house, fully satisfied and clutching an armful of fat sticks, I scrambled to the top and prepared to jump down, then noticed two large black cars coming along from the direction of the station. Better wait until they had passed. Then as the first limousine drew opposite to me, a lady in the back, wearing a large hat, its brim turned back from her face, leaned forward, smiled and waved a gloved hand. Without thinking, I waved back, almost losing my precious sticks as I did so. Then as the cars proceeded towards Jurby, I realised who I'd seen. The Queen Mother, as she was to become, noticing a lone child balanced precariously on a field gate in a quiet country lane, had waved and smiled. It may have been an automatic reaction, but it delighted me – a smile and just for me! The Royal visitors had been making their way to the aerodrome to inspect RAF personnel, before boarding a Dakota at three o'clock to return to London.

I only ever saw one other 'important person' in

Sulby and that was three years later when Lord Montgomery, the Commander of the Eighth Army, was made a Freeman of the Borough of Douglas. I stood with others outside the Sulby Glen Hotel and watched him salute as he was driven past, standing up in the Land Rover he was travelling in. I have to say I didn't really understand the reason for the visit.

In 1945 the summer ended on a high note when, on 15th August, Japan finally surrendered. Ellan Vannin, of course, had its share of church services, parades and street parties. This time the sun shone and at night the skies were alight with flares and bonfires. Sulby's celebrations were in the Church Hall with games on a nearby field, but Mother and I had small explosions of our own, only they were not fireworks. We were sitting at ease in the kitchen before going down to the Hall, when suddenly – Bang! There was first one and then another explosion outside.

'Ye Gods! Whatever's that?' Mother leapt to her feet. Hurrying out of the back door, we were met by an all-pervading smell of alcohol coming from the shed.

'The Rhubarb!' Mother exclaimed. 'The shed must've got too hot. Oh, damn it!'

Earlier in the summer Mr Caine had given us some rhubarb, too much for us to eat, so never one to waste anything, Mother had decided on a wine making experiment. She'd hoarded enough sugar, got yeast from the baker and all went well. The recipe book said, '… the longer it is kept, the better is the wine.' So all three bottles had been stored in a corner of the shed with the coal. Now two had exploded in the summer heat. Like a fire fighter tackling an incendiary device, Mother gingerly loosened the top on the remaining bottle and we surveyed the damage: liquid alcohol and broken glass everywhere. That was the end of wine making for a while.

It had been a momentous year one way or another. The Internment camps had closed; soon the Air Force would leave Andreas, and Jurby would change from an RAF Bomber Command Training School to an Officer Cadet Training Unit (OCTU). The islanders looked forward to shipping links being restored to their pre-war level, although until 1946 Fleetwood and not Liverpool continued to be the port of call for Steam Packet boats. Visitors began to trickle back, albeit with their ration books, but that didn't make any difference to us. Aunts Det and Connie visited us briefly, but it became apparent that Mother had no intention of returning to England with them.

It was in the following spring that I became an official member of the Church community. This was Ethel's idea. We stepped cautiously into the kitchen one Saturday just before tea.

'Mother, Ethel's had an idea,' I began. Mother cradled the loaf she was cutting against her chest, the bread knife poised in mid-air.

'Yes?'

'Er…Can I start Sunday School tomorrow?'

In the light of this unexpected request, Mother set both bread and knife down on the table in front of her. Sandwiches could wait.

'What's brought this on?'

'Well,' I turned to Ethel hovering behind me and she took up the cause.

'Well, it's the Sunday School Picnic in July,' she explained. 'We'll go out to places on a chara and Ann could come if she went to Sunday School. She'd like it,' she added lamely.

'Yes, all the kids go. Please, can I go too?'

Mother thought for a minute then retrieved her loaf. 'Well, if you really want to and if it's alright with the Church, I don't see why not.'

So on Sundays I sang hymns, learned prayers, illustrated Bible stories, wondered at the fragile thinness of the pink-edged pages of the Holy Book and, with the others, waited patiently for July and our earthly reward. The war over, the island woke to its summer season when there would be visitors to entertain once more. At last I was to see more of Ellan Vannin and realise that my world was not confined to our village, Ramsey and Douglas. And as I came to know the island which had become my home, I would grow to love it and claim it as mine, even though I was not Manx born.

'Can I wear my white cardigan? It'll match my sandals.' Weeks before the Picnic I was planning what to wear. The sandals were new, not the usual brown children's sandal, but much more adult – white slingbacked, with a wedge heel about an inch high and best of all, peep toes. Already their pristine canvas had been cleaned with Blanco, that special paste out of a tube, which gave off a puff of white powder if you'd used too much and stamped when it was dry. I was grown up and ready to go on the first of my 'Church Picnics'!

Leaving parents behind, we gathered in the chill of a summer morning outside St Stephens and waited for our 'chara'. It was a thirty-five seater, no on-board hostess or toilet of course, though it did have a somewhat stained carpet; and there were ashtrays on the back of each seat, their dusty smell mixing with peppermint or pear-drop, or whatever sweets the travellers had saved up for. Clutching our sandwiches and bottles of pop, we chattering Sunday Schoolers clambered aboard, the boys rushing to the back seat, the rest of us squashing in, hoping to sit with a best friend. The adult organisers always had the best seats at the front near the driver.

We were too busy anticipating our destination to pay much attention to the island's natural beauty on the way, but those who'd been before might soon recognise where we were.

'We're going to Peel Castle!' came a voice as a small island across a sandy bay came into view.

'Woo-ooo!' Howling from the boys at the back. 'Do you think we'll see the Moddy Dhoo ?'

'What?'

'The ghost of a fierce black dog,' moaned the boys. 'It's always there and if you see it in the guard-room, it means you're going to die,' and they howled again.

Peel Castle stands on St Patrick's Isle near Peel harbour. It is an imposing place, its heavy curtain wall of red sandstone built to encircle and protect the now ruined buildings within. Even as children we could sense its long history. The Isle, only about seven acres

*Peel Island, full of history, with ben varrey sporting
in the waters beyond.*

in size, had been inhabited from pre-historic times.
Flint implements had been found there; it was attacked
during Viking raids; it was the centre of early
Christianity and in the 11th century it was the ruling
seat of the Kingdom of Mann. Looking through tall
arched windows, all that remained of St German's
Cathedral, you could see the sea on one side, and
against a backdrop of hills, the kipper factory and the
town itself on the other. Soon, clinging on lest we fell
down the rocks, we skirted the path outside the thick
walls, and made our way to the tiny Fenella beach
nearby which nestled beside a small hill. We only had
time to climb its foot and as we struggled upwards,
seagulls screeched overhead and shells crunched
beneath our feet. Some of these Scallop shells (known
locally as Queenies) were intact and I took a big one
back for Mother. It served as a soap dish in the scullery
for a long time. We also picked sea pinks and delicate

harebells (Fairy Thimbles or Mairanyn ferish), which wilted before we had even scrambled back aboard the coach.

We left Peel and on the road to Douglas, those at the front stood craning their necks to see ahead.

'Can you see St Trinians? Is the roof still gone?'

Then, as we passed the roofless ruins of a small church in a field beside the road, Ethel flopped back on her seat and told me the story of the wicked goblin of St Trinian's. A Buggane, a fearsome creature who could change his shape, would let nobody re-roof the centuries old church.

'They tried to put the roof on loads of times,' she said, 'but he kept blowing it away. Then one day a tailor said that when another roof was on, he'd stay in the church all night to stop the Buggane. If he could finish a pair of trousers before daylight, the roof would stay on. Well, he stitched and stitched, and he'd nearly finished when he ran out of cotton. So he ran to get some more, but when he got back, the Buggane was back, and he was so mad that he blew the roof right off again and the tailor was blown away as well.' She sat back and nibbled half a biscuit lingering in her pocket. 'That church will never have a roof now, you know.'

I remembered that Daddy had said that the Island was magical, and it seemed that there were enough fairy stories to make that true, and even if the tales were just superstition, it was wise to go along with them, 'just in case.' Few Manxmen will cross the white stone Fairy Bridge at Ballalona, between Castletown and Douglas, without nodding and bidding 'Good day' to 'the little

St Trinian's Church shows what a wicked Buggane can do.

people'. Sometimes known as 'themselves', they, the Phynnoderee, are shy but quixotic creatures. They live in ferny dells and are partial to a dish of milk which, I was told, a few older Manx still left in the hearth or outside the door for them. On the other hand there are other fairies, glashtan, who are mischievous, loving to tip things over, turn milk sour or make the chimney smoke. The tarroo-ushtey is a water bull said to live near water in glens, but I didn't ever hear his story – or see him.

A coach trip into Douglas could end with a visit to the Manx Museum, where we tried in vain to comprehend the past; or to Nobles Park to expend our energy in the play areas, or better still, to the northern end of the promenade and Port Jack. There, after fish and chips in Kelly's Café set back against the foot of a rocky cliff, we went on to the White City amusement park on Onchan Head. Looking down over the two mile sweep of hotels and boarding houses along Douglas Bay, we enjoyed candyfloss and ice cream and the usual stalls, hoopla and hook-a-duck, throw the darts and rifle shooting, always a hit with the boys. If we were very brave, we might even try the Ghost Train. Then home at last amid much singing, generally One Man Went to Mow, Ten Green Bottles or Coming Round the Mountain.

Another venue might be Castle Rushen in the south of the island, a solid medieval building of blue-grey limestone, beautifully preserved and overlooking Castletown harbour.

'Look, the clock's only got one hand,' someone might say looking up at the time on the castle's clock tower. But that was how it had always been. Still kept in working order and wound every day, the clock was reputed to have been a gift from Elizabeth 1st in 1597. Over the centuries this castle had been a prison, an asylum, army barracks and the centre of the island's justice system. But for us the most interesting aspect was daring each other to go down into the dungeon. The other place of interest nearby was not the old House of Keys, the original site of legislature until 1869, when Castletown was still the capital of Mann, but a place in the square where, it was said, the last witch on the island was burned to death. We stared at the spot, trying to imagine it.

'I s'pose she put the evil eye on some fella, made things go bad for him,' someone remarked. 'It can be done, you know. People still do it. Ugh! Race you to the chara!'

Just over two miles from Castletown, returning

home via Foxdale (nothing to do with foxes, the name derived from fors-dale, valley of the waterfall), was Silverdale Glen, and the coach turning in that direction brought cheers from all young travellers. Silverdale was an ideal venue for our picnic, sometimes taken on a grassy area beyond the lake, where we could play games if we wanted to. But the lake itself held more appeal for it had pretty coloured pedal boats. We had to be dragged away from those and by then we had worn ourselves out pedalling and our clothes were patterned with water splashes. There was also a little roundabout of wooden horses uniquely driven by a water-powered wheel, but it was not always working.

The Sunday School Picnics opened my eyes to just

how much Ellen Vannin had to offer, so many places of beauty and historic interest. And all of these places, and more, I knew I'd visit again one day with Mother, for I remembered something she'd said after the brief summer visit from my aunties. We were ambling down the middle of the road with Ruff as usual, when after a long thoughtful silence she said, 'You know, I think we'll just stay here after all, because we're used to it now, and anyway you'll be going to the Grammar School in September.'

Ready for secondary education.

Chapter 12

It was an accident of fate that the end of the war more or less coincided with my departure from Sulby School into the wider world of Secondary Education in Ramsey. In the spring of 1945 I had passed the Scholarship, which enabled me to attend Ramsey Grammar School, but to Mother's disgust, my entry was denied. The pass numbers had been higher than the allocated places and so, because I was younger than many of my peers, my entrance was held over to the following year.

'We'll see about that,' declared Mother, but it was a battle she couldn't win. It also happened that in 1946, Ramsey Grammar School, founded in the eighteenth century, was to become, along with a school in Douglas, a 'pioneering multilateral school'. A letter informed us that I would therefore be a pupil who would 'have the opportunity of taking the course best fitted to his or her bent or ability' and that all pupils would be 'equal in status irrespective of the kind of course they take'.

In effect, it was the beginning of the comprehensive system, and we were the guinea pigs, although the Grammar School would keep its name and its motto, 'nil amanti difficile' (nothing is too difficult for those who love). We were 'streamed', the curriculum planned to suit each form, with the emphasis on academic or more practical work as required. I was in the A stream and in one case at least, know that the theory worked in practice. Stanley, from a neighbouring village, started in the D stream, but gradually climbed to an A, finally leaving for university and an important job in the nuclear power industry.

So we found the money to buy the new uniform and I prepared to sally forth; but first, 'Try it on,' said Mother, 'and let's see what you look like.' I took the clothes into her back bedroom, while she sat on my bed gazing out of the window. I wore the lot – the long-sleeved white blouse and green and yellow striped tie; the bottle green, box-pleated gymslip with its low-slung belt; long thick black stockings bought for the winter term and dreadful thick, regulation bottle green knickers with elastic in each leg – and all topped by a matching green blazer and beret which I hated because it would never sit at an attractive angle.

'I'm coming,' I called as I walked up the hall and into the bedroom. Mother turned, her jaw dropped and she fell back on the bed and laughed and laughed.

'Oh dear,' she gasped at last. 'Look at those stockings!'

* * *

So in September 1946, shortly before my twelfth birthday (which made me six months older than the average age of the thirty three pupils in my form) I trotted down to the station in defiant white ankle socks, with a new brown canvas satchel and not a little trepidation, to catch the 8.14 a.m. train to Ramsey. A ten-minute walk from the station brought us to our new educational home in the further of two school buildings several hundred yards apart. The original Grammar School was for senior pupils, but for the first three years everyone else settled in the newer building, completed in 1939 but used during the war by the Air Ministry as an RAF Control Centre. As memories of primary school rapidly faded, I spent all day away from home, enjoyed a hot school dinner (5d a day at the beginning) and returned to Sulby on the ten past four train each evening.

Life expanded in all directions – new friends, more sports, homework that piled higher with the years and mixed classes. Oh, the excitement of little SWALK notes (sealed with a loving kiss!) passed surreptitiously along the rows during lessons – 'Will you come to the pictures with me on Saturday?' – or of seeing an idolised senior boy coming towards you, even though he didn't know you existed. Year in, year out, we pattered along the path between one building and the other. The girls played tennis, hockey and netball and we all tried to uphold the honour of the school in the island's inter-school sports. We broke the rules and sneaked into town at lunchtime to buy sticky chocolate buns from a cake shop near the corner of Parliament Street, and caught up on homework as we rattled along on the morning train. My secondary school years were very happy ones and I recall not only a new circle of friends but some members of staff who eventually became friends too.

Miss Eyles was a rotund and benign Latin teacher, who trod slowly and heavily into the room on our first morning intoning, 'ambulo, ambulates, ambulant' – the only Latin I can remember. We had two French teachers, Miss Stephenson very thin and precise, and as Senior pupils, Miss Battle a strong, outgoing woman who successfully taught me to read and to think in French. It was in Miss Stephenson's class that the translation of the word for pavement sent John J. into peals of infectious laughter. 'Trottoir', he hooted hysterically, 'le trottoir,'- a word we would all remember as we joined in his laughter. Miss Kewley bustled round the Domestic Science room showing us how to iron handkerchiefs precisely and when teaching us how to fry chips, quoted a golden rule which still echoed round my head as I cooked them years later – 'Twice into the fat – once to cook and once to crisp and brown.'

'Come on, Smiler, try again.' That was how Mr Norris, our gentle Maths teacher, addressed me during the first years as I battled with geometry. But in the end he gave up, for I couldn't draw a straight line even with a ruler. Our Senior Maths teacher, Mr George, who also happened to be a fearsome Headmaster, did not succeed with me either. He was so deep into his subject that he couldn't understand anyone not knowing what Maths was about.

'Anyone can do Maths,' he once roared at me, and I was very glad to prove him wrong when I failed the O level exam. I also failed in Geography, too, but that was because Mr Shimmin was so handsome. He had the longest, darkest eyelashes I had ever seen, and I spent most of his lessons gazing at them and not at the books I should have been studying.

Miss Williamson was a much-loved History teacher, deeply immersed in her subject and an avid reader of the Manchester Guardian. She was sufficiently relaxed with senior pupils so as to sit back and close her eyes whilst marshalling her vast army of facts into orderly and interesting ranks. Then eyes still closed, she dictated notes, conducting her thoughts with an aimless waving of the arm. Many of her pupils stayed in touch with her into adult life and I was one of them, and she used to pass on our 'old scholar' news in the school magazine, 'Y Feeagh', (The Raven). She rejoiced in her nickname, 'Squee', a word derived from her first name, Louisa – 'Louisa Squeeza'. I visited her occasionally until she died in her 95th year and dedicated a book to her.

But the master for whom I had the greatest respect and affection was Ken Garwood. It was 'KG' who introduced me to the music of Gilbert and Sullivan when I took part in his production of 'Trial by Jury'.

But more importantly, it was KG who gave me a lasting love of English literature as he strode up and down the aisles, passing on his knowledge with enthusiasm. It was on a school trip with him to Stratford on Avon at the end of May 1950 that I was away from home for the first time and saw my first Shakespeare plays. The 'Lady of Mann' took us to Liverpool from where our coaches seemed to take us on a tour of England before arriving at a Youth Hostel in Stratford. By then I must have been in a daze, for I remember nothing of the play we saw that evening. But the next day, after taking in the Stratford sights, the matinee performance of 'Julius Caesar' was a revelation – the power, the colour, the story itself. I was entranced, even though I didn't know then who Anthony Quayle (Caesar) and John Geilgud (Cassius) were. The trip ended that night with coaches back to Liverpool and a rough crossing on the midnight boat best forgotten.

The 'Sulby Gang' in Stratford on Avon – from left: Gladys, the author, Letitia and Florence

The author with classmates and revered English teacher,
Ken Garwood.

It was KG, too, who at the end of June the following year, was responsible for organising our two day school visit to The Festival of Britain on London's South Bank. We stayed the night in large converted air-raid shelters in South Clapham – mine was called Jellicoe – with rows of beds, concrete walls and steps leading back up into the fresh air. Again we took in plays at the Old Vic and the Stoll Theatre, Kingsway, but the Festival was an unforgettable, once in a lifetime experience. It all seemed so modern and out of this world, especially the new Festival Hall, the Dome of Discovery, bewildering in its displays, and the Skylon by the river bank. Made of steel, like a tall thin cigar, its tip nearly 300ft high, it appeared to float in space. Then when we got nearer, we saw that it was supported on almost invisible spider-like legs, so that you could look up to its base about 50ft above your head. We marvelled at the towering fountains, the crowds, the wonders of television, the many exhibitions, the spectacle of 'ordinary people … celebrating peacetime …and giving themselves a pat on the back', to quote the post-war Labour minister Herbert Morrison – and all for an entry fee of just two shillings (10p!). We would have needed a week to see it all. It was almost too much for a child from Sulby. I slept for eighteen hours after the journey home but the adventure had been worth it, and I knew I was lucky to have Mother who scrimped and saved to fund the trips, and KG, our wonderful teacher. Sadly, this inspirational man died only a short time after his retirement and I can't be the only one who, while regretting his going, would be ever grateful for being fortunate enough to have known him.

Life was not all centred on school, although I did join the school lunch-hour Ballet class. I was too old to ever become accomplished, but I enjoyed the music and the grace of the movements. I continued with GFS and spent time with Jean and my old and newer friends. But now that coaches took to the roads again during the holiday season, Mother and I realised that here was the opportunity for us to get to know Ellan Vannin better. So occasionally on a summer's day we pretended we were holidaymakers and went on organised coach outings – afternoon or evening 'mystery' tours, or occasional 'Round the Island' day trips. It was the only way for us, without transport, to visit parts of the island we had never seen.

It was on a Day Trip that our Manx education began. The coach began by taking us south and practically the length of the island to Cregneish, an open-air folk museum with panoramic views, where crofters had lived for centuries. Reached by a very steep road, which made the engine strain and splutter, we arrived at the top of the hill to find a group of old white-washed cottages set behind dry stone walls. Some needed attention, but most were well thatched.

Entering one cottage, the only house open to the public, we stepped straight into the past and on to the hard clay floor of a room divided into two by a wooden partition. The larger side, to the right, was the kitchen (thie mooar) and there on the chiollagh, a hearth of large stones set on the ground, a turf fire glowed – the Manx names were there for us to see. Our eyes stung as its smoke, choosing to leave by the open door rather than a hole in the thatch, drifted round the room. To the left a ladder reached up to a small bedroom (cuillee) the wooden floor of which stretched over part of the room we stood in. It was a home about as basic as one could get.

'Well,' murmured Mother as we left to watch chickens scratching in the grass opposite, 'We can't complain about Scacafell now, can we?'

We felt at home with the chickens, even the pigs,

but didn't much care for the Manx Loaghtan sheep nearby, a breed over one thousand years old and rarely seen anywhere else. The name denotes the colour of their strong wool – lugh mouse, dhoon brown, – but it pays not to get too close to their long curling horns – the ram has four. We stood to clear our lungs of turf smoke and from our vantage point we could see the southern most point of the Island, the Calf of Man, and that was to be our next destination.

Soon we were gazing across the Sound, treacherous waters which swirled between the mainland and the little rocky island known as the Calf, owned by the National Trust and preserved as a bird sanctuary.

'Oh,' said Mother, as her hair blew wildly round her face in the salty wind. 'This will do us good. Breathe in!'

A leaflet provided by the coach driver informed us that 'Calf' originated from the Scandinvian 'Kalfr', meaning a small island lying beside a larger one, (which was logical); and that a lighthouse, one of three, set precariously behind it on Chicken Rock, was near the deepest part of the Irish Sea. 'Well, I don't think we'll try swimming across to that then,' Mother added as she tried to fold the leaflet against the rush of a mischievous wind.

'Well ladies and gentleman,' said the coach driver as we hurried back to the shelter of the vehicle, 'I know you'll be wantin' a cup of tea, but don't worry. We're going to Rushen Abbey now and you'll get one there.' He heaved himself into the driving seat and added over his shoulder, 'It was once the home of Cistercian Monks and though there's not much left of the Abbey now, they do make a good cup of tea and home made scones – and strawberries and cream.'

He was right, and sitting beneath overhanging vines we soon revived and smiled to hear visitors from our coach pronounce Ballasalla, where we were, as Ballasall-ar. We felt smug because we lived on the island and we knew how it should be said!

'It says here there's a very old bridge over the river,' said Mother, consulting the leaflet again. 'Let's see if we can find it.' So, having bought a little china tub of jam made from apricots grown against the old Abbey walls, we drifted over to the Silverburn River, tree-lined and aptly named as it glided serenely over clearly visible stones. 'Isn't this pretty?'

Together we leaned on the wall of the narrow, sun-dappled Monks' Bridge. Just over three feet wide, hump-backed and more than six hundred years old, it seemed to breathe its history. As modern voices faded, one could imagine the sound of packhorses on the cobblestones, when, centuries ago, the Monks left to visit their outlying lands and travellers from the outside world came to the Abbey – a monastic medieval life so far removed from our modern twentieth century. It was so peaceful and relaxing that we really felt as if we were on holiday. Many of the island's seventeen national mountain or coastal Glens, which we discovered on other tours, had the same effect. Most were much smaller than our Sulby Glen, but all had a kind of quiet magic: narrow paths winding between steep wooded sides, and little bridges over fern hidden streams, most of which eventually tinkled their way out to sea.

Occasionally we found that an evening Mystery Tour wasn't such a mystery after all, but that didn't matter. We were exploring somewhere we'd never otherwise see. We once left Ramsey and travelled past Scacafell to wander through the countryside until we arrived at the Point of Ayre, the flat, northern most tip of the island. We gazed up at the first of two lighthouses standing among rare lichen, heather and short, yellow gorse, then went nearer the sea to find the second, much smaller one, standing in isolation on the sand. Wind and tides had moved sand and shingle to extend the shoreline, so it had been added thirty years after the first one.

'Let's see if we can find treasure washed up on the shore,' suggested Mother, and we wandered among the pebbles and watched oyster-catchers who seemed busy doing the same thing. I found a fat, curiously shaped piece of wood, about three inches long. Looked at one way it resembles an open-mouthed fish, turn it and it becomes a cockerel with an upstanding comb. Then, on the way home we passed occasional thatched cottages in narrow lanes, which we hadn't even known existed.

As pretend holidaymakers, we once joined a coach which went south to Port Erin and Port St Mary, both small ports and popular holiday destinations. In Port Erin we dodged puddles in the Marine Station and Fish Hatchery and wondered at the tiny fish in their tanks. Then coming out into the sea air again, we joined the coach driver leaning against the vehicle. We followed his gaze across to Bradda Head, its craggy rocks from which copper had once been mined, rising steeply out of the sea.

'Looks like a key, don't it?' The driver nodded in the direction of a tower, which stood on the Head. 'Built in memory of a fella called Milner who was very good to Port Erin folk– last century, that was.' The building did look a bit like a fat key upside down. The man screwed up his eyes against his cigarette smoke. 'He was rich, they say, made his money from safe-making in Liverpool, came to live here and that's supposed to be like the key to the first safe he made.' And having given us a potted history of a local landmark, the driver flicked his cigarette butt into the water and added, 'Come on then. I think we're all here now. We'll have a look at Port St Mary and then go round Castletown and on to Derbyhaven.' It was as well we didn't have to give him directions for we had no idea where we were going.

Derbyhaven proved to be a sheltered bay about two miles from Castletown. The coach stopped on the Langness peninsula, from where we could look across to Ronaldsway airport and King William's College, a prestigious school for boys. At the northern end of Langness lay a small island reached by a narrow causeway.

'Now,' said our knowledgeable driver standing on the coach's doorstep, 'Langness is where the first Derby horse race was held. The 7th Earl Derby started it about 1630 and the 8th Earl wrote the rules himself in July 1669. Only horses bred in the island could race and the prize was worth £5 – a lot of money in them days. It ran here 'til the Derby rule ended in 1756. So you see our Derby race was first because the Derby at Epsom didn't begin until the late 1780s. I'll bet you didn't know that!' He hauled open the door and stood aside. 'There you are. I know there's a golf course here, but you've no time for that today!' He grinned. 'You can walk over to St Michael's Isle. It's been a place of religion and battles for our land for centuries. Back in half an hour please.' So we walked among the rank grass and harebells and explored what was left of a tiny, Celtic chapel, once restored, but roofless for at least 300 years, and stared at a round defensive fort, built with a birds-eye view of the sea.

'This wall must be about eight foot thick,' said Mother, staring up at it. 'And look, there's a gun still there.' Then she yawned. 'Sorry, must be all this sea air. Come on, let's go back.' And as we settled in the sun-warmed seats of the coach, she added, 'It's been a good day out. I reckon we'll sleep well tonight. We must do some more of this!'

Chapter 13

We didn't always rely on coach trips for our 'holiday jaunts'. Occasionally in summer we left Ramsey aboard the electric railway to follow, more or less, the east coast of the island as far as Douglas. This was a vintage Victorian journey. The carriages were original, the 'newest', we learned, coming into service in 1906, and it ran along what is still the longest, narrow 3ft gauge track in the British Isles.

'Oh, let's go on the toast-rack!' exclaimed Mother ignoring the closed carriages to climb with some difficulty into a high open-sided one. 'We'll see better there.'

She was right and we breathed in country and sea air throughout the journey. Bench-like seats were set behind each other in two rows, open to the elements on the outsides of the car, though there were heavy wooden blinds which could be pulled down if the weather got too much. It was a trip best undertaken on a warm day. Considering it was a journey of only eighteen miles, it took a long time, but it was great fun and since the scenery was wonderful, it would have been a pity to hurry. Sometimes the train hugged the coastline, sometimes it creaked and swayed through the fresh, green countryside, past hamlets and glens, stopping frequently for its passengers and ending the journey with a harsh screech of brakes at Derby Castle at the northern end of Douglas promenade. Whereupon the backs of the seats were swung to face the return direction, ready to take travellers home.

During the summer months there were similar 'toast-racks', this time horse drawn, to take one along the length of the Douglas promenade. Pulled by patient horses, travellers could stop the tram, within reason, more or less where they pleased. Mother had a passion for horses, sometimes even in her sleep. 'I dreamed of my brown horse again last night,' she'd say, but we never worked out why she had this repetitive dream. Although Daddy had been a horseman, she had never been near one, except to pat a nose or feed an apple. So the horse trams were her delight and whenever possible we had to sit beside the driver.

'It's an awful lot for them to pull,' was her first remark as she watched the horse strain forward to begin pulling a tram-load of people. 'How many trips do they do?' She seemed happier when she learned that there were enough horses to ensure that each one only did three or four return trips each day. 'And what do they do in the winter?'

'Oh, they're well cared for,' answered the driver. 'They have their holidays then, just graze and please themselves. And when they grow old,' he added, anticipating Mother's next question, 'they go to the Home of Rest for Old Horses at Bulrhenny. That's just on the outskirts of Douglas.' That was to become Mother's favourite destination when, later, she could afford to travel about more.

Apart from seeing a horse tram for the first time, Douglas was the scene of two other new 'after war' experiences for me. One was a sunny matinee visit to the Gaiety Theatre and the other, more mundane, was eating a peach afterwards as we walked along the promenade. I'd neither seen nor tasted one before. I wasn't sure about the furry texture of its skin, but the flesh tasted wonderful and it helped complete a lovely day out. I had found the Theatre breath-taking, even though I didn't know then that it was designed and opened in 1900 by Frank Matcham, (the Victorian architect responsible for both the Coliseum and the Palladium in London). I was dazzled by its ornate decoration, its statues and, above all, the colourful Act Drop Curtain, with its swirling girl dancing for her Sultan.

The show was pretty unbelievable too – were those 'Soldiers in Skirts' really men? Later we were to make other summertime theatre visits and enjoyed comedians like tall thin Nat Jackley who seemed to be made of rubber and Norman Evans with his 'over the

The unique, carefully restored exotic Victorian Curtain,
the only surviving example of William Helmsley's work.
With thanks to the Gaiety

garden wall' gossip – all matinees, we never saw
Douglas in its night-time glory.

On other occasions we went on the bus to Peel and
discovered what I hadn't seen on the Sunday School
trip – houses nestling together along little narrow
streets which led down from the centre to the sandy
seafront, the sure mark of a town where the sea
provided a livelihood. We watched fishing boats leave
the harbour to put out to sea and other fishermen
sitting patiently along the breakwater, rods aloft,
waiting for a catch. Over all was the pervading smell of
wood smoke and kippers. We watched 'mermaids'
playing in the water behind the castle, while others,
perhaps, saw seals and porpoise. Sometimes we sat

eating ice-cream on the promenade, on forms which, when Manx was being revived in the future would invite people to:

'soie sheese, gow dty aash, as bee jee booisal'

'sit down, take thy rest, and be ye thankful.'

And then on the journey home, we'd turn in our seats and look back to see the glorious sunset, which gave Peel its name of 'Sunset City'. And it was a city, small though it was, because St German's on St Patrick's Isle was a cathedral, ruined now, but the only one Ellan Vannin had.

It was while we were in Peel one midsummer that we saw a notice leaning against a rather old coach which advertised an afternoon trip to Tynwald Hill in St John's just over two miles away.

'Tynwald Hill? That's where they read out the new laws on July 5th every year isn't it?' said Mother.

'Yes, in Manx, English and in German,' I replied to show that I'd learned something in school.

'German?' echoed Mother. 'Are you sure? Why German?'

'I don't know. Someone told me.' It was some time later that I found out that 'in German' was a joke. Tynwald Hill stands in the parish of St German – so the information had nothing to do with the language. There were other typically Manx jokes specially designed for the unwary, like 'Which do you like best, a kipper or a smoked herring?' and at first I was caught out by them all.

Anyway, on the day in question, Mother said, 'Oh, we ought to go there. We really should know more about the island's parliament.' Mother loved to go somewhere new. I'm sure she would have travelled the world had she ever been given the chance.

St Johns itself proved to be a small village, and Tynwald Hill man-made, fashioned it was said by soil from each parish on the island, and brought here because it was approximately the centre of the island. Consisting of four platforms, with a base circumference of 256ft, the whole thing rises to a height of 12ft (so an informative board in the nearby Church told us.) It also informed us that Tynwald came from the Scandinavian 'Thingvollr' meaning Assembly or Parliament Field.

'I didn't expect to learn so much today,' remarked Mother mildly as we stood looking up at the Hill, trying to imagine what it looked like on Tynwald Fair Day.

It is on the top circle that dignitaries sit beneath a cone-like canvas roof. They include the Lieutenant Governor representing the Crown, the Lord Bishop and the Deemsters (Judges) who read out the new laws for all to hear. There is no excuse for anyone present not knowing the law. This formal ceremony is preceded by a service and a procession behind the Sword of State from the church to the Hill. Originally rushes from every parish were strewn along the path, thereby ensuring that those involved in law making had symbolically walked all over the island with the laws. Business done, everyone enjoys festivities, the market and sideshows which always were part of this public holiday. 'I'd like to see it one day,' said Mother, but she never did – although in my teens, as a member of a Manx Folk Dance group, I danced at Tynwald.

Turning our backs on parliamentary things, we then faced Slieau Whallian, a natural hill over 1000ft high and clad entirely in pine trees, and I remembered my fellow Sunday Schoolers calling it the Witches' Hill. In days gone by, the story went, anyone thought to practice the Black Arts was rolled from its top in a barrel lined with spikes, on the grounds that only a witch could survive. If she did, she was put to death, if she didn't she mustn't have been a witch after all. There was never a winner.

Mother relaxing on St Patrick's Isle, Peel.

It was in 1947 that I first became aware of motor-cycle racing. Most who hear of the Isle of Man immediately think of motorbikes and the Tourist Trophy races. I didn't, and since racing was abandoned during the war years, there was no reason why I should. I didn't know what to expect when the TT began again in 1947. I just welcomed days off from school, because roads round the circuit were closed, and that included the main road to Ramsey, which passed RGS. That hadn't been the case when racing first began over a shorter track near Douglas in 1904, and there are hair-raising stories of riders having to dodge early morning fish carts and other road users during practice sessions. However, by the time I first experienced the smell of Castrol from a racing bike, Ellan Vannin had organised its life round road closures, so that competitors could hurtle round the 37¾ mile circuit several times in June and again in September for the more amateur Manx Grand Prix.

'Let's go and see what it's all about,' said Mother when we heard there was to be an afternoon practice session. 'If we stand behind the school railings we should be alright.' So before the roads closed we duly stationed ourselves in front of Sulby School. In the distance came the dull growl of a Norton bike. Then suddenly it roared past so suddenly and so fast, that I was round the back of the school with my hands clamped over my ears before I knew it. We realised then that the Straight was indeed the fastest stretch on the course. Gradually, as bikes continued to roar past, I ventured forth and by the end of the practice was used to the noise and converted to the TT for the rest of my life.

In subsequent years Jean and I spent many hours among the crowds perched on a wall facing the vicious right hand bend of Sulby Bridge, at the end of the Straight and a few yards from her house. We saw riders successfully change down from high speed to negotiate the turn, and we saw others who failed, hit the bridge wall and bounced into the road. We collected autographs from riders who had stopped, and admired their machines even though they'd broken down. Harold Daniel won that first post-war Senior race at an average speed of 82.81 mph over seven laps of the circuit – and that was fast! From then on 'the Races' slotted into our calendar each year and we admired Geoff Duke, Freddie Frith and other riders who, as technology improved got faster with the years. Later, in a new century, a Suzuki Superbike with an exceptionally skilled rider would lap at more than 128 mph. By then the Straight would have is own speed trap, which in 2008 would see Bruce Anstey touch 190 mph near the school. Fortunately, during a race, there's never anything coming in the opposite direction.

So an interest in motorcycles surfaced twice a year, and for the rest of the time contact with the world away from Ellan Vannin came through wireless and film, and letters from pen-pals (one French, one American, but they didn't last long). I became a fully-fledged film fan, sending off for signed photographs and falling in love with stars like young Richard Attenborough, Laurence Olivier, Cary Grant and Gene Kelly – I would have given the earth to dance with him! But they all lived on the silver screen. It never occurred to any of us that we too might one day be able to join the world of the performing arts by becoming, if not a star, an actor.

But watching Fred Astaire and Gene Kelly during my secondary school years fuelled my interest in the hobby I was desperate to pursue – ballroom dancing. Dancing of all kinds it seemed (I learned tap briefly before the war) was in my blood. Two of my classmates, Paula and Josie, went dancing on Wednesday and Saturday at the Pool Ballroom situated at the end of the Mooragh promenade. I wanted to join them when there was a late bus back, but 'No', Mother put her foot down. But I was older now and becoming more independent, so sparks began to fly. Even though in the late forties and early fifties, there was no such thing as a 'teenager', I believed I was old enough to have my own way.

'No,' said Mother firmly. 'Schoolwork comes first. There'll be plenty of time for dancing when your exams are over.' I argued, I sulked, I stormed into my room, threw things around, frightening Ruff, so that he cowered under the bed until it was safe for him to appear again. Then as I wept at the injustice of it all, he soaked up my tears in his forgiving fur. I even tried cajoling and promising to work harder, but I wasted my time. Once a decision was made, ice formed and there was no way of thawing Mother's determination. So I had to be content to live through each week without the glamour of ballroom dancing. When I was old enough to see sense, I had to admit that she'd probably been right. I did well in the exams, passing five O levels, A level English in one year's study, and in the following year achieved passes in Scholarship English and three other A levels at grades sufficiently good for me to enter University, although in the end I didn't. But around the time of these squalls, there was George and for a while his presence made for even bigger storms.

Shortly after I entered the Grammar School, Mother began to go to village Whist Drives and it was there that she met George. He was a bachelor, about her own age, typically Manx, hard working, unforthcoming, but naturally taking her side in an argument. To my shame, I must admit that I was jealous of his being around, breaking up the partnership that Mother and I had built over the years. And he didn't like cats. How could anyone decent not like cats? That put him at a disadvantage for a start and to make things worse, he was full of Manx superstition. He pottered in one Sunday morning just as Mother, having thrown down used tea leaves on the narrow carpet in the hall to 'settle the dust' as was her wont, began to sweep them out towards the door. Needless to say, all cleaning involved a brush. We had no vacuum cleaner.

'What are you doing?' he exclaimed. ' Don't sweep the luck out, woman. Sweep it the other way. Haven't you had enough bad luck?'

I resented him 'first footing' on New Year's Day, or being 'qualtagh' as the Manx say. Wasn't I dark enough to bring luck as the first person to enter the house in a new year? He frowned when I proudly brought in early daffodils.

'Those shouldn't be in so early,' he said. 'The goose hasn't her goslings at her yet. If she sees them in the house, she'll leave the nest.'

Since when, I thought, has a daffodil looked anything like a gosling and we had no geese anyway! But apparently I'd brought in bad luck, as I would have done had I gathered hawthorn flowers. I think even the slow speech of this Manxman annoyed me, and the unusual turns of phrase. By 'at her' he meant 'with her', and the Manx will not go to look for something, they'll see if they 'can put a sight' on it. As for these superstitions, they may have been old, but they had no logic.

But 'You have your friends and I'll have mine,' said Mother firmly, so I just had to swallow my resentment. In the end, we silently agreed to put up with each other and when I was fifteen George offered to take me out on the back of his 250cc motorbike before TT week so that I could see the Course in its entirety. It was a sedate and enjoyable outing on a warm evening in late May and the views were breathtaking from the mountain stretch of the course, but I could appreciate how thrilling it must be at speed. We were within two or three miles of home on a straight and empty stretch of road beyond Ballaugh, when we came upon a car creeping along at snail's pace. George pulled out to overtake it – or began to – but just as we passed, it swerved straight into our path. There was a bang and I found myself rolling in the gutter, cutting my head and filling my knees with gravel. At last, peering round the back of a policeman who appeared from nowhere, I could see George spread-eagled in the road. He was unconscious for four days, and all because the woman driver sneezed, or so she said.

In Ramsey Cottage Hospital I gripped the policeman's hands and screamed, as what felt like acid was poured into raw wounds, so that a nurse with a small nailbrush could literally scrub gravel out of my knees. Then I was taken home to my white-faced mother. Our own doctor arrived and discovered a deep two-inch wound on my hip, by then a lurid green with dye from the regulation school knickers. It would have been stitched had the hospital staff bothered to examine me. As it was, the doctor slapped the contents of a tube of penicillin over it, put on a dressing and crossed his fingers. 'Let's hope that does the trick,' he said. It did heal eventually, leaving a scar as a souvenir. But two days after the accident it took more than three painful hours to soak off and replace the bloodstained bandages on my knees, while the roar of practising motorbikes echoed along the Straight – though by then my face had become so swollen that I wouldn't have seen them anyway. I haven't been on a motorbike since, though I've never lost my love of watching them. My shredded headscarf was unwearable, my ballet days were over, and the relationship with George cooled as the years went by. But there were other people to take my interest.

Chapter 14

It was Jean who took me on my very first 'sleepover' away from home. We were about twelve and we went by bus to her Grandmother's house in Laxey on the east coast, about fifteen miles away from Sulby. Part of the route went round Bulgham Bay, at that time a long, narrow curving bend, with high rocks on the landward side and a deep drop to the sea on the other. To us, sitting on the bus's front seat upstairs, it all looked very dangerous and we clung to each other as we swayed precariously close to railings to gaze down into the waters below. It all added to the excitement of a weekend away from parents.

Nanna, a widow, was a tiny, spirited old soul with wild grey hair. She lived in a little cottage set high behind a wall and reached by a dozen narrow steps rising from the main Douglas to Ramsey road. From its perch, one looked down towards a valley where from the mid 1800s zinc and lead had once been mined.

'Just in time' she said the first time I stepped shyly through the front door behind Jean. 'You can take our lad his tea, he's home from hospital now. He won't be going back.' She took a cup and saucer from a table by the kitchen window and thrust it into my hand. Jean came to my rescue.

'I'll show you,' she said and propelled me towards a closed door on the other side of the tiny hallway, adding, 'It's my uncle. He's got TB.'

A thin man, pale and tired, lay back on a narrow bed beneath the window. He grinned and held his hand out for the cup. 'So you're Jean's pal,' he began, then pulled himself up abruptly, pointed to the bedside table and began to cough. The cup was hurriedly deposited and I felt Jean pull me out of the room as Nanna bustled in, clucking anxiously. Then the door closed on mother and son and I didn't see him again on that visit, or ever again.

This was the first of many weekends in Laxey, all of them happy. The old lady enjoyed our company and made no concessions to our being there. We were expected to help her round the house, but we could come and go as we wished, so long as we were home in the evening by nine o'clock.

'You can make your own tea,' she said as she poked the fire on that first visit. 'I'm not going to wait on you. What's the use of having a dog and barking myself?'

She grinned a gummy grin and sat back heavily in her fireside chair. She always sat there after meals and snored gently while we washed up the dishes in the back scullery. Tea was the always the same. Jean and I made sandwiches with sweet home-grown tomatoes liberally dusted with pepper, and I don't think I have ever enjoyed tomato sandwiches as much as I did then. At night we climbed into a high double bed in the second little bedroom and sank down into a mountainous feather mattress to whisper well into the night. We knew we'd be wakened early when Nanna appeared at the door.

'Time you were up, girls,' and she would hand us cups of tea, sweet and so strong that I swear a teaspoon could have stood upright in the cup. Jean shared her Nanna with me because I didn't have one at home and I soon shared more of her relations too.

'Let's go up to the Wheel,' Jean said, referring to the famous Water Wheel, sitting high above Laxey or 'Laxa' (Scandinavian, meaning salmon river). The Lady Isabella, with a diameter of seventy-two and a half feet, is the largest working water wheel in the world, although it had become just a tourist attraction after the mines it pumped water from closed in 1929. At their peak in the mid 1870s, these mines, the deepest in the world at 1500 feet below ground level, produced as much zinc as all the other mines in Britain put together. So, as it was a nice day, the decision was made and we wandered across the electric train lines towards Ham and Egg Terrace. This was actually called Dumbell's Row, after the Victorian Chairman of The

Laxey Mine Company. But some houses in the terrace had at one time become tea-rooms, providing meals for those toiling up the steep road, as we were doing, to see the Wheel. From that day I came to share Jean's Uncle and Aunt and their three sons, who were about our age.

They lived near the Wheel and knew everything there was to know about it, and later I visited them on my own for many years. I was always greeted warmly and made to feel part of their family. I formed a strong lifetime friendship with them all, always leaving with a great bunch of prize Dahlias from their garden when they were in bloom. That first day Jean and I climbed all 95 steps up the Wheel's once elegant spiral staircase to admire the view and look down on the Wheel itself.

We did that often over the years, especially if it was turning. We loved to watch diamonds glistening in the

The author shares a view from the Wheel with her mother, 1950s.

water as it splashed round. We walked miles with the boys, sometimes among gorse and bracken on the hills beyond the Wheel or through Laxey Glen Gardens; sometimes down to Laxey's pebbly beach, talking, teasing, always having fun. They once threatened to make us walk to the top of Snaefell with them, but needless to say, we never did. Nor did we use the electric railway, which would have taken us the four mile journey there from Laxey station. So although we looked down on the countryside from the top of the Wheel, we never stood together on the island's highest point to view the six kingdoms around us – England, Ireland, Scotland, Wales, Mann and the Kingdom of Heaven. We were happy enough having fun in the kingdom of Mann.

Another of Jean's cousins, a few years older than we were and also destined to become a lifelong friend, sometimes came from Liverpool during the summer to visit Nanna. We enjoyed Vic's visits, for he danced ballroom. He took us out and treated us like grown-ups. We danced in the little Pool Ballroom in Ramsey, or more often went into Douglas on the bus. There we'd find our way to the Villa Marina, with its lovely dance floor beneath the octagonal roof, or the beautiful Palace Ballroom, said to have one of the largest parquet floors in Europe. It was certainly heaven to dance on. We'd begin the evening up in the balcony, looking down on dancers swirling round the white-gloved MC in the centre of the ballroom. But soon the rhythm of the music drew us down to the floor to take part in the magic, while the immaculately dressed band played on the stage above us.

We didn't then realise how lucky we were to dance to musicians like Joe loss, The Squadronnaires, Ted Heath or Ivy Benson and her band. In later years, I often went dancing with other girls and we never lacked for partners – that was how one socialised then. It all felt so romantic, but there in the fifties, our teenage friendships were innocent, alcohol was never part of the evening, unless it was a Babycham, and then only if it included a cherry on a cocktail stick! In our circle we admired and treated each other as equals, holding hands, giving goodnight kisses, but for us there was never anything more sexual to it than that. In our book, that was for the future. We were in no hurry to grow up and get serious. We were having too much fun. Mother understood this and was happy for me to go out at weekends, generally to the pictures, if she knew who I was with. So I worked hard at school, played too, and life moved along placidly until I was seventeen. Then, by a twist of fate, I met Nicky.

It was a completely unexpected, chance encounter and it took only one heart-stopping glance of mutual recognition to bring us together. It was as if it was meant to be, as if we knew each other already. We met whenever we could, occasionally during the week and in Ramsey at weekends. But as our precious time together slipped away and even though Mother disapproved, we became very close. All too soon my tall, brown-eyed Air-force Cadet from Leeds had to leave Jurby as a Pilot Officer, and move on to continue his training. Before he could join Fighter Command he must learn to fly all types of aircraft, and flying was his joy. As he moved from base to base, from Bulawayo in Rhodesia to Norfolk, Doncaster and Devon in England, his letters were full of it. '…learning aerobatics now…' '…start on jet-fighters soon…' ' … take you above the clouds one day…' So over the months we wrote regularly, as winter turned to summer again and we planned to meet as soon as we could – hopefully in Cambridge when I started college there in September. In the meantime, opportunity, money and the Irish Sea were keeping us apart and we both had a full study programme – at one time he had fourteen subjects on his syllabus. Then there was a gap of a few weeks without a letter, but I knew he was moving on to a new station, and would be writing when he was settled. And I had his photograph in my pocket, so he was always with me, even in school.

It was the first week of June, almost time for my final exams. I arrived home for tea to find a letter addressed to 'Ann'. I stood in the front room and tore it open and my body drained. Wordlessly, I handed it to Mother. After a minute, she handed it back, then turned towards the kitchen saying quietly, 'Just be glad you weren't married.' And that was all. Nicky's mother had written returning my last letter and informing me that at the end of April her son's jet fighter had gone down in the Bristol Channel. Nicky was '…missing, believed killed.' My other half was gone. It was as if a favourite book had been snapped shut half way through the story and there was no way I could ever open it again. Lamartine, in his poem 'L'Isolement' said how I felt better than I ever could:

'Un seul etre vous manqué, et tout est depeuple.'

History had repeated itself and I was too grief stricken to think how it must have affected Mother. '… and I won't be the only one' she'd said to her sisters in June eleven years earlier, but she could never have known how close to home that would be. How could lightning strike twice like this? This was life, not a novel. But apart from my closest friends, nobody knew what had happened. Nobody knew that someone else who was or had felt part of my life would become just another name on a Forces' Memorial. Almost overnight I learned the art of containment. I could almost see an invisible, protective wall building up before me. I moved on, of course I did. After all, my childhood had been a lesson in how to do that and life went on, didn't it? I went on to have a successful career, I dated, I married, had a family of my own and divorced. But always, when a jet plane splits the air overhead, I must stand and watch it. My heart leaps, I feel that ache inside and I'm eighteen again.

A few weeks later, in 1953, as Captain of a Games House, a Prefect and Deputy Head Girl, I went tearfully along to my last School Assembly to join in singing the school song – 'Forty Years On', a song shared with Harrow and other Grammar Schools. I had been very happy at RGS. In a few weeks I would leave Ellan Vannin, my home and my friends, to start a new chapter in England, where I would train as a teacher. It was to college rather than university that I went, even though I had the necessary qualifications for the latter. With the help of KG and the staff, I'd worked out that

I would be several thousand pounds better off if I began teaching in two years rather than four or five. I wanted to be the breadwinner in my family now, to give back something to the parent who had given so much to me, and I wanted material things too. In the event, those two years at Homerton College, Cambridge, affiliated to the university and the best training college in England, I was reliably informed, would prove to be happy ones and the beginning of my 'moving on' with my life.

The end of August saw a whirl of packing. The bulk of my belongings were being sent on ahead, carefully packed into an old tin trunk, second hand, of course, and much more used to travelling than I was. All too soon came the morning of my departure. The night before had brought stormy winds whistling round Scacafell and tossing the trees.

'Oh, don't worry,' said Mother as we sipped our night-time cocoa. 'It'll blow itself out.' I wasn't so sure though it had calmed down a little by the time we got up. An early breakfast was forced down before we hesitated at the open door.

'Ah well,' said Mother stepping outside at last, 'We must away and grovel in the mud,' – another of her odd phrases, always used when she was reluctant to do something and always guaranteed to bring a smile, however rueful. So we struggled to the station with my suitcase.

'Off, then,' said Fred and he pulled at the first pipe of the day, persuading it to breathe out that lovely aromatic smell that we associated with him. 'Aye, aye.

See you later, then', and he struck another match and ambled back into the shelter of his waiting room.

Sitting facing each other in the chilly train, Mother and I rattled along at seven o'clock in the morning, trying to ignore the fact that we were soon to be parted, and instinctively knowing that things would never be quite the same again. Near Kirk Michael I caught a glimpse of the sea in the distance, and saw that the waves were 'white horses'. Not a smooth journey after all then. Later, as we steamed past the turning stone, Mother wondered if it would turn for us today and I duly laughed and told her she was talking nonsense as usual. But deep within the hollow feeling inside, I wondered if it might indeed have turned to face the sea by the time I returned home. After all, the island was unique in so many ways.

An hour later we set off along Douglas harbour, a tiny lady beside a tall innocent, struggling in turns to carry the suitcase. Joining the slow shuffle of other cold travellers, we reached the quayside's covered way and saw the Steam Packet boat looming over us. Tearfully we parted – 'See you Saturday,' a farewell we used because it made parting easier. So although Mother and I knew that 'Saturday' was months, or later even years away, that was how it always was. If I'd been by her side when she died, which sadly I wasn't, I know I'd have whispered as she slipped away, 'See you Saturday.'

Slowly the boat turned its face toward Liverpool and we slid past the iconic Tower of Refuge in Douglas Bay. Far from being the fairytale castle I had once thought it to be, I now knew it to have been built in the 1830s by Sir William Hillary, founder of the National Lifeboat Institution. It stood as a haven for anyone unfortunate enough to be wrecked on the dangerous Conister Rock which lurks there beneath the sea. It was then that I realised that this was the first time I'd made this journey on my own. I was stepping into another world now, passing through Mannanan Mac Lir's protective mist, invisible though it might be this morning. I was moving on to a life of new and as yet unknown and very different experiences: Cambridge, its magnificent colleges and the beauty of the riverside in all seasons; college life and interesting new subjects to study; many new friends, especially Polly with whom at first I was to share a room and who became very dear to me over the next half century; music with 'the chaps' in Caius College; my first 'bottle party' at St John's, and a May Ball there with champagne and dancing till dawn and a midnight supper of roast Swan (for which that college has special dispensation); my first experiences as a teacher …

I looked back to watch Ellan Vannin fade into the distance. It was still beautiful, even without sunshine and as it grew further away I could imagine the rocky cliffs and sandy beaches, the gentle hillsides and secret glens and the miles of soft green countryside, where I'd learned so much about the important things in life and the pace at which it should be lived. The Manx anthem's '… gem of God's earth …' with its '… sweet mountain air.' was not such an exaggeration after all. I may only have spent a few years there, but they were formative ones and I had been given a relatively carefree childhood in a time of war. I loved the place. It may only have adopted me as a 'comeover', but now it was my island. And this journey back and forth across the Irish Sea was one I was destined to take many times over the following years. Happily, I would see much more of Ellan Vannin!

Epilogue

~~Forty~~ Fifty years on …

$\mathcal{A}$nd of course I did see Ellan Vannin again. After college I taught in London's East End, and then returned 'home' to teach in Andreas School until I left to get married. Then, as my husband climbed his professional ladder, I found myself living in England, Ireland, Scotland and Wales and wherever we lived I joined a drama group, either as actor or director! As my two sons became older I returned to teaching, ending up in the English department of a Secondary School, until I took early retirement and turned to writing.

But more than fifty years after the Isle of Man first

became my home I took a holiday there on my own, unable to believe that half a century had passed. We had, of course, spent family holidays with Mother in Sulby where, through sheer hard work, she'd established a small café in a large house at the end of the Straight. At that time, however, I'd been so caught up with our lives that I'd looked at once familiar places without really seeing them. Then as the twentieth century neared its end, with my sons grown up and Mother no longer with us, I decided to go back to Ellan Vannin. I wanted to savour it alone, at leisure, and see how much it had changed, if at all.

I stepped down from the plane at Ronaldsway (by far the best way of crossing the sea!) and breathed in the pure Manx air. It seemed fresher than anywhere else, but colder than I remembered. I saw that tourist attractions like Rushen Abbey and Castle Rushen had been brought back to life very effectively. Then, driving my hire car through to Douglas, and remembering to say good-day to the little people at the Fairy Bridge, I found that the island's capital appeared more crowded and commercialised than I remembered. The main streets looked familiar but the policemen showed their Manx individuality by wearing white summer helmets. Leaving behind fine new houses, and estates scattered where green fields had been, I found myself back in the countryside, following the coastline through Laxey to arrive in Ramsey. It was a refreshing drive, with less, more leisurely traffic than in England, all roads in good condition, many of them bordered by trees and hedges.

In spite of more housing, Ramsey appeared much

the same, and although the Plaza cinema, once my place of romantic assignations, was now an empty space, the electric train station still stood beside it. A large new supermarket had appeared not far from the now defunct steam railway station, but Mooragh Park was as I remembered it, with boating lake, palm trees and bright flowerbeds. As was to be expected, the nature of some of the shops had changed. This was especially true of the cobbler's shop at the end of Parliament Street, its display still so clear in my memory. Although apparently dedicated to fast food now, it looked neglected. Foolishly I felt a pang that the window, which had reflected the shattering of my family, should now bear only fly-specked adverts for American style hamburgers and 'donuts'.

At last, with some trepidation lest it be 'spoilt', I drove out to Sulby. Arriving by car was not so much fun but sadly, the northern part of the railway system is no longer in operation. Gone forever are the busy little Manx steam trains, unless you travel between Douglas and Port Erin in the south as a summertime holidaymaker. The old red-circled crossing gates had been preserved a short distance from their original moorings and a 'Public footpath' sign pointed along the railway track, but it was too over-grown to venture in. Our railway station had been renovated and extended to become a dwelling, its windows draped with impenetrable cream net curtains. I felt acute disappointment that I couldn't retrace my steps across the dusty waiting room or step back into Fred's cosy little office where ashes dropped softly from his ever-burning fire. Much as I would have liked to see just how successfully this part of my history had been brought into the present, I felt I really couldn't knock on the door. However, Fred himself had not entirely disappeared for his son ran his mother Maggie's shop at the crossroads. It appeared to be a busy place, with customers forming a queue before it opened, perhaps because it is the post office too, since little Florrie had long ago fluttered off to a more hallowed perch. Opposite the shop, the Sulby Glen Hotel and its neighbouring cottage were still there, but not the house from where Eunice rushed out so fatally. That space formed an extra entrance to the pub car park.

Leaving the car by the station gates, I retraced steps taken thousands of times up 'the lane', now boasting a raised footpath where tar once bubbled through the gravel. A few new houses had bobbed up in peaceful fields, but the old homes were still there, pristine and neat, beside tall hedges and grass verges frozen in time. And there was Scacafell. It appeared to have been refurbished, externally at least. The old gate had finally collapsed and the front path, now running at an angle from the road, led to the front door, which sheltered from the winds beneath a glass and concrete porch. The occupants enjoyed electric light, the house, beneath a new roof, didn't seem to frown any more and the front garden appeared handkerchief sized – although of course, it hadn't shrunk. I had grown. Lingering only for a moment, lest I was observed and I wasn't ready for that yet, I continued to retrace our walks toward Jurby. Nothing seemed to have changed until I reached 'the smelters', where the first of two surprises awaited.

Tree stumps and nettles, whispering ghosts and piles of rubble had gone, to be replaced by a neat red brick bungalow, aptly named 'Newholme'. Where tangled weeds had bent in the wind, there now blew a line of washing – shirts and baby garments and a child's nightdress bearing the legend 'Bedtime Elves'. I wondered if the new residents ever heard ghostly sighs from the old smelters' elves.

But Julia's old cottage held a bigger surprise, a testament to changes wrought by imagination and a healthy bank balance. Gone were the sweet-smelling, full-blown roses and hens scratching in the mud. The two cottages were now one and a large window stretched across Julia's front door. A long lounge told of internal walls knocked down and much work done within the shell, along with an extension, complete with bow window and French doors, at the end furthest away from Julia's muddy garden. And behind all these windows, a myriad of glass ornaments sparkled in the sunshine. George's little stream had been banished beneath determined concrete, so that it now trickled through subterranean soil instead of gurgling happily across the scullery floor. I wondered what he and Julia might have thought at seeing a modern 'For Sale' sign valuing their home at £175,000.

I wandered on past hedges of hawthorn and willow vying for space above yarrow, cow parsley, sweet honeysuckle and foxglove. I saw again bramble and dog rose and the ubiquitous yellow cushag (ragwort) among softly swaying grasses. Occasionally meadowsweet tossed its feathery head inviting me to smell its honey perfume and I remembered dire warnings about the effect it may have. The road to Jurby was still largely empty, save for a new white line hesitantly stretching away into the distance. But where was the cotton grass where Dorothy sat reading? Only clumps of spikey marsh grass defied unwary sheep trying to nibble it. Gone too, was 'the plantation'. Cut down long ago, it no longer sighed its secrets and one would never know that it had ever been there. Time to turn back and retrieve the car.

Leaving quiet lanes behind I reached the aero-drome, no longer home for planes or their aircrew. Airport buildings had been joined by a small housing estate and the hangars now housed small businesses – sign writers, woodworkers, antique dealers. A notice above the entrance to the Officers' Mess, where I once danced in my late teens, proclaimed 'Welcome to Jurby Hotel'. The main attraction appeared to be an enormous Junk Shop set among the hangars opposite – somewhere to idle away a wet afternoon, I'd been told. 'Jurby Junk' is a treasure trove owned by Stella, a charismatic lady who bobs up between the shelves where least expected. There could be found anything from odd postcards, books and records to stuffed animals, wool and toys. Strange costumes hung from the walls. Piles of dusty china and glassware teetered on shelves above old-fashioned pans, cutlery and rusty paint tins. This place would be a godsend to any theatrical props man. Several people wandered round, rootling among the merchandise, but how much was actually bought, I would never know.

After so much dust it would be nice, I thought, to visit again the beach where Jean and I spent so many happy hours playing in the soft sand – I might even paddle, just for old times sake! But as I walked down the path leading to the sea, the air became contaminated and I noticed an unpleasant smell. The gate we used to climb over in excitement now bore an officially typed and commanding notice:

Note: This beach and waters are contaminated with raw sewage.

Turning away quickly, I left with a heavy heart. Is this what 'progress' meant? I felt sad, and sorry for today's youngsters who may have progressed technically, who think they have freedom, but who could no longer enjoy an innocent and totally carefree childhood like ours. I could only hope that the Manx government would very soon clean up this part of the island.

Since I was in Jurby, I returned via its Church on the northwest coast to visit my father's grave. Standing on a rise, St Patrick's can be seen for miles around, long, once white painted, at one end a tall tower, which appears to lean, as if keeping an eye on the sea gradually eroding the coastline below. It was as I expected, silent and lonely there, my father's headstone, shared with a crew member, as pristine and desolate as when it was new. A few harebells blew in the wind, but there was sadness in the air and the church, open though it was, was cold and uninviting even on that sunny day.

I drove slowly on along quiet country lanes and found again another church I remembered, old St Mary's near Ballaugh village. Cycling out there with school friends, I'd been fascinated by its long history, the changes wrought by centuries, and especially by the old stone gateposts, which still leaned drunkenly towards each other. In this churchyard there was a special old gravestone half hidden in the grass, where Ann Ellison, aged 'about 24 years' had lain since July 1654. We used to try to imagine her life and made up stories about her and as I looked for the grave, I still wished I knew more.

On then to join the TT course at Ballaugh Bridge, where racing motorbikes literally leap into the air, and on to arrive full circle back in Sulby again. Turning right towards the Glen I passed the new, purpose built primary school. My old school, empty now, looked much the same as it always did but Pop's haven, the schoolhouse, had been demolished. The Claddagh didn't seem to have changed much, although it is now an accepted campsite and tent flaps fluttered in the breeze. Above the Claddagh the irregular outline of Primrose Hill looked down implacably on unfolding history as it had done for centuries; and I imagined I saw ghostly figures tumbling and shrieking down its slopes in fun.

As I wandered round the village, Snaefell stood in the background, a symbol of permanence on an island which in spite of itself is slowly changing – will have changed again, perhaps, by the time these words are read. This is inevitable, I suppose, as new ideas and technology filter through to even the most independent island. I saw that Jean's old home was still there as was the Mill, though apparently clouds of flour had given way to its own Kella brand of whisky. Occasionally I passed villagers and saw again the smile or nod, or was bid good-day, just as I had been so long ago. The 'locals' hadn't changed, but then, perhaps they never really do in rural areas. The ghosts of childhood drifted about me. I could hear them in the soft Manx drawl of those I spoke to and fifty years melted away. I still love my island, and I'm grateful for the memories which Ellan Vannin guards for me, for as long as I wish to remember them.

Ann Moore graduated from Cambridge in 1956 and became a teacher, first in London, then in various schools in her adopted home of Worcestershire. She was also very active in amateur theatre, directing, writing or acting in over seventy plays and establishing a community drama group in her home village.

In later life she turned to writing, always her first love. She published numerous non-fiction titles (including Curiosities of the Isle of Man), and spent her final years researching an ambitious historical novel set in Elizabethan England.

She died on September 27th 2014, just one day short of her eightieth birthday.

Printed in Great Britain
by Amazon